Simple Natural Crochet

Simple Natural Crochet

Timeless patterns for accessories, clothes,
and the home, made in beautiful natural yarns

Susan Ritchie & Karen Miller
of Mrs Moon

CICO BOOKS
LONDON NEW YORK

This edition published in 2025 by CICO Books
An imprint of Ryland Peters & Small Ltd
1452 Davis Bugg Road, Warrenton, NC 27589

www.rylandpeters.com

10 9 8 7 6 5 4 3 2 1

First published in 2017 as *Simple Chic Crochet*.

A CIP catalog record for this book is available from
the Library of Congress.

ISBN: 978 1 80065 402 0

Printed in China

Editor: Kate Haxell
Pattern checker: Jemima Bicknell
Designer: Vicky Rankin
Photographer: Penny Wincer
Stylist: Jo Sawkins
Illustrator: Stephen Dew

Art director: Sally Powell
Production controller: Mai-Ling Collyer
Publishing manager: Penny Craig
Publisher: Cindy Richards

MIX
Paper | Supporting
responsible forestry
FSC® C106563

Contents

Introduction

We love crochet! When we had our yarn store we were very much a knitting AND crochet retailer, not mainly knitting with a little bit of crochet on the side. Some of this was because—quite handily—one of us (Susan) is very much a crochet-er and the other (Karen) a knitter, although we can both switch between the hook and needles if necessary. However, the main reason for our dual yarn-craft approach was the huge increase in interest in the art of crochet. We were inundated week after week with people wanting to learn this lovely craft.

There are a couple of stumbling blocks with crochet though. One is that it's that bit trickier to learn than knitting. Whether this is because most people have a go at knitting as a child but maybe not crochet, or if it's because crochet is just a bit less intuitive, I'm not sure, but it certainly seems a little harder to get to grips with. The other issue is that crochet can have a tendency to look a bit… well… too crocheted. Lacy, great! Textured, great! Overly crochet… hmmm… we're not sure that always works. So we've tried to create designs that are not only reasonably simple, but also look rather lovely and "not too crochet."

Crochet can be just as versatile as knitting and we hope that we've demonstrated that here with a huge variety of garments, accessories, and home decorations. And in many ways, once you have mastered the basics of crochet, it is much more straightforward than knitting. As well as written patterns we have included charts where appropriate, as we find them very helpful for more complicated designs—you can see exactly where each stitch is supposed to go.

We have been lucky enough to be able to use some of the most luxurious natural fibers and we would encourage you to find the best yarns you can for your lovingly made projects. But if you can't find the exact yarn we used, or can't justify the cost, then please don't be put off. All the projects include the gauge (tension) of the yarns used so you can substitute any of them.

If you are a beginner, start with one of the blankets, either the camping throw (see page 70) or the bedrunner (see page 52), or if you'd prefer a smaller project, the hot water bottle cover (see page 60) is super-simple, too. There are lots of easy-to-read instructions on techniques at the back of the book, and check out online resources or our own website, www.mrsmoon.co.uk, for videos. One word of warning, make sure you know whether you are watching US or UK tutorials; some of the same stitch names describe different stitches, which can be very confusing!

We hope you are inspired by our designs; we've loved creating them and hope that you do, too!

Susan and Karen xxx

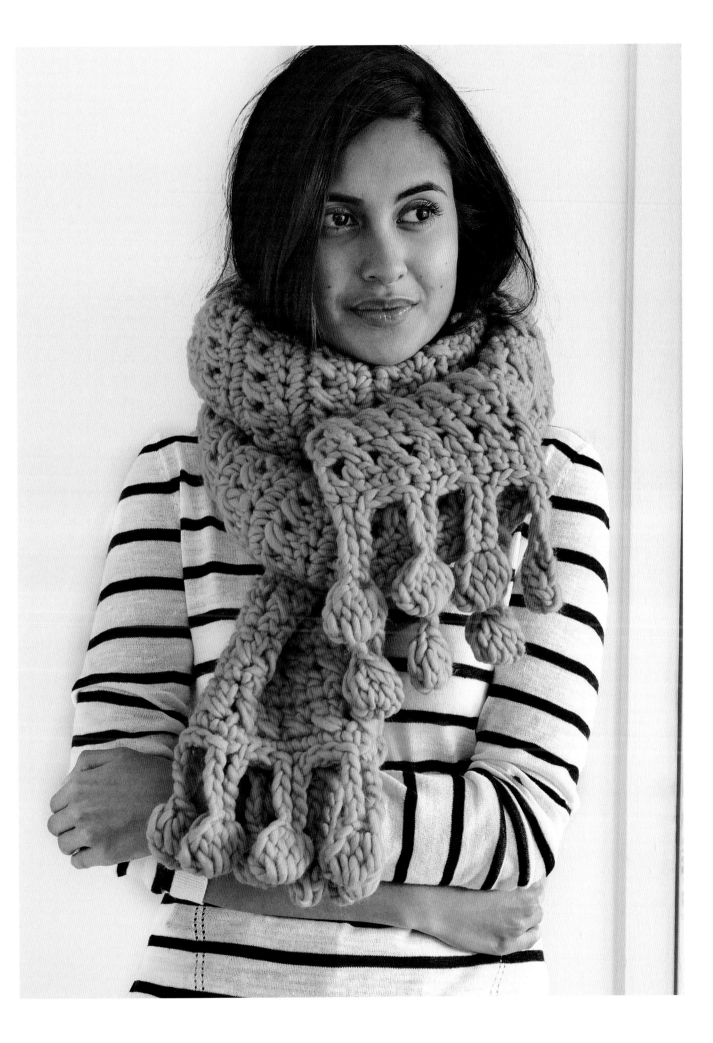

CHAPTER 1
To Wear

The idea of crochet garments might evoke scary thoughts of frilly bed jackets and terrible tabards, but actually crochet can be used to make elegant, easy-to-wear items that will become wardrobe staples. And as crochet is so easy to work, the projects in this chapter will grow encouragingly quickly.

GRANNY SQUARE *Coatigan*

When I was planning this fabulous cardi/coat, I was thinking about how garments made of granny squares (or actually any crochet), can be amazing or slightly mad... I hope that I've achieved the amazing category here! This coat swings out beautifully when you walk because of the way it has been constructed, and it has three-quarter-length bell sleeves to give it a sophisticated edge. The coatigan is super-simple to create because you just need a lot of the squares! Once you've made them all, sew them together as shown, then add the all-important collar and front band that finish it off beautifully.

Yarn

Mrs Moon Plump DK (80% superfine merino wool, 20% baby alpaca) light-worsted-weight (double knitting) yarn, 1¾oz (50g), 125yd (115m) skeins

3(4) skeins in Rhubarb Crumble (A)

3(4) skeins in Cherry Pie (B)

15(19) skeins in Blueberry Muffin (C)

Hook and equipment

US F/5 or G/6 (4mm) crochet hook

Size

To fit: S/M(M/L)

Finished measurements

Chest: 34½(51)in (88(130)cm)

Length (nape to hem) (including border but not collar): 34(34)in (85(85)cm)

Gauge

Each square measures 4¼in (10.5cm) using US F/5 or G/6 (4mm) crochet hook

Abbreviations

PUFF = [yoh, into st, yoh, pull back through st] 3 times, yoh, pull through all 7 loops, to secure puff yoh, pull through loop on hook.

PUFF1 = This is a puff at the beginning of the round, the ch2 counts as one stitch so you work this as a puff but work two instead of three reps (5 loops on hook), yoh and pull through to secure.

See also page 114

SQUARE

Color 1 is A or B, color 2 is the one not used, color 3 is C.

S/M Make 40 squares with A as color 1, and 40 with B as color 1.

M/L Make 55 squares with A as color 1, and 55 with B as color 1.

In color 1, ch5 and join with a sl st to form a ring.

Round 1: Ch3 (counts as 1dc), work 15 more dc into ring, join rnd with a sl st into top of ch 3, fasten off color 1. *(16 sts)*

Round 2: Join color 2 to any dc from rnd 1, ch2 (counts as 1hdc), PUFF1 into same space, work 1 PUFF into next dc and into every dc to end of rnd, join rnd with a sl st into top of ch 2, fasten off color 2. *(16 puffs)*

Round 3: Join C to any space between puffs, ch3 (counts as 1dc), dc3tog into same space, yoh and pull through to secure, ch1, *dc4tog into next space between puffs, yoh and pull through to secure, ch1; rep from * to end of rnd, finishing with a sl st into top of ch 3.

Round 4: Sl st into next ch 1 space (this is where you need to start this rnd; you may need to sl st twice to do this neatly), into this ch 1 space work (ch3 (counts as 1dc), 2dc, ch2, 3dc) for corner, do not ch1, *3hdc into next space, 3sc into foll space, 3hdc into next space, ** and into next space work a corner (3dc, ch2, 3dc); rep from * twice more and then work one final rep, finishing at **, join with a sl st to top of ch 3, do not fasten off.

Round 5 (sc round): Ch1, 1sc into same space, 1sc into each of next 2dc, work 3sc into ch 2 corner space, cont working 1sc into every st, and 3sc into every corner space around, finish rnd by joining with a sl st to top of first sc, fasten off.

TO MAKE UP

You can sew the squares (and the seams) together. However, I have crocheted them together by slip stitching them (see page 123). I find this quicker and easier as I am very bad at sewing; it is also easy to pull back if you go wrong.

To join the squares, first arrange them (see diagrams on page 12). Right sides together and slip stitching through the back loops only, join squares to form long strips. Then join the strips together.

	B	B	B	B	
	B	B	B	B	
	B	B	B	B	
	B	B	B	B	
	B	B	B	B	
	B	B	B	B	
	B	B	B	B	
	SH			SH	
	F			F	
S	F			F	S
S	F			F	S
S	F			F	S
S	F			F	S
S	F			F	S
S	F			F	S

SL	SL	SL
SL	SL	SL
SL	SL	SL
SL	SL	SL

	B	B	B	B	B	B	
	B	B	B	B	B	B	
	B	B	B	B	B	B	
	B	B	B	B	B	B	
	B	B	B	B	B	B	
	B	B	B	B	B	B	
	B	B	B	B	B	B	
	SH	SH			SH	SH	
	F	F			F	F	
S	F	F			F	F	S
S	F	F			F	F	S
S	F	F			F	F	S
S	F	F			F	F	S
S	F	F			F	F	S
S	F	F			F	F	S

SL	SL	SL
SL	SL	SL
SL	SL	SL
SL	SL	SL

Size S/M

Alternate the color centers throughout.

Back (B): Lay out a rectangle four squares wide and seven squares long.

Shoulder (SH): Add one square at each end of the top row of four squares.

Front (F): Attach a strip of seven squares lengthways to each shoulder.

Side panels (S): Attach a strip of six squares to each front panel, aligning the bottom edge of the strip with the bottom edge of the front.

Fold the coatigan in half across the middle of the shoulder squares, so that the bottom edges of the back and the front/side pieces match. Join the top two squares of each side panel to the aligning squares on the back (these will be the second and third ones down from the top). Leave the lower part of each side seam open as a split.

Sleeves (SL): Lay out a rectangle four squares wide and three squares long. It's easiest to fit the sleeve into the opening before joining the underarm seam. On the wrong side, join the sleeve squares to the top of the side panel, the single front square, the shoulder square and the topmost back square. Then join the underarm seam.

Size M/L

Alternate the color centers throughout.

Back (B): Lay out a rectangle six squares wide and seven squares long.

Shoulder (SH): Add two squares at each end of the top row of six squares.

Front (F): Attach two strips of seven squares lengthways to each shoulder.

Side panels (S): Attach a strip of six squares to each front panel, aligning the bottom edge of the strip with the bottom edge of the front.

Fold the coatigan in half across the middle of the shoulder squares, so that the bottom edges of the back and the front/side pieces match. Join the top two squares of each side panel to the aligning squares on the back (these will be the second and third ones down from the top). Leave the lower part of each side seam open as a split.

Sleeves (SL): Lay out a rectangle four squares wide and three squares long. It's easiest to fit the sleeve into the opening before joining the underarm seam. On the wrong side, join the sleeve squares to the top of the side panel, the single front square, the shoulder square and the topmost back square. Then join the underarm seam.

EDGING

Round 1: Using C, work a rnd of sc all the way around the edge of the coat, working 3sc into every corner st (at the bottom edge of each split and at the bottom edge of each side of the front opening), and at each side of the back of the neck (where the front joins the back) and at the top of the split on the side seam work sc3tog as a decrease around the corner.

Rep rnd 1 once more.

Round 3: Work a further rnd of sc just around inside of opening, working sc3tog either side of back neck, fasten off.

COLLAR

Row 4: Using C, work sc around neck (left SH square, two squares of back neck and right SH square), working sc3tog in corners as for edging, turn.

Row 5: Ch1, 1sc into same space and 1sc into every st to end, working sc3tog in corners, turn.

Rep row 5 twice more.

Row 8: Work sc into every st, do not work sc3tog in the corners, turn.

Row 9: Ch3 (counts as 1dc), 1dc into next sc and into each st to end of row, increasing by working 3dc into each corner st, turn.

Rep row 9, 6 times more.

Row 10: Neaten edge of collar with a row of sc starting at the edge of the collar (where it meets the button band) and working evenly up the edge (as a general rule work 2sc down the side of each dc), then work along the top and down the other edge, working 3sc into each front collar point and back neck corners, fasten off.

LEFT-HAND BUTTON BAND

Row 1: Join C to bottom LH corner, ch1 (does not count as st), 1sc into same place, 1sc into every st up to st before the collar starts, turn.

Row 2: Ch1 (does not count as st), 1sc into same place, 1sc into every st to end of row, turn.

Rep row 2, 3 times more.

Fasten off.

RIGHT-HAND BUTTON BAND

Row 1: Join C to st next to collar at top of RH edge, ch1 (does not count as st), 1sc into same place, 1sc into every st to bottom, turn.

Row 2: Ch1 (does not count as st), 1sc into same place, 1sc into every st to end of row, turn.

Rep row 2, 3 times more.

Fasten off.

Weave in ends (see page 125).

Block coatigan following instructions on ball band.

Making squares

I find it easier making all the circles first (rounds 1–3), and then working rounds 4–5; I guess I get into a rhythm. I also weave in the ends as I go as this can become an almost insurmountable task if left to the end…

CROCHET *Skirt*

Crochet is, for many garments, quite tricky compared to its close cousin, knitting. Garments just tend to work better with the close fabric that knitting creates... I spend quite a lot of time trying to make my designs look not "too crochet"! However, the crochet skirt is the big exception! Knitted skirts can be heavy and cumbersome. Crochet creates gorgeous shapes and lace that swings fabulously and really flatters the feminine form. So, here is my first crochet skirt. I'm so pleased with it. It sits on the hips and has no tricky openings to deal with, and it gradually flares out with simple increases in the lace pattern. I urge you to give it a go... your friends will be begging you for one!

Yarn

Cascade Ultra Pima (100% pima cotton) sport-weight (double knitting) yarn, 3½oz (100g), 220yd (200m) skeins

5(6:7) skeins in Taupe 3759

Hook and equipment

US F/5 (3.75mm) crochet hook
Large tapestry needle

Size

To fit: S(M:L)
Finished measurements
Waist: 30¾(32½:35)in (78(83:89)cm)
Length (waistband to hem): 19½in (49cm)
Waistband depth: 2¼in (6cm)

Gauge

14 sts and 8 rows over dc sts in waistband using US F/5 (3.75mm) crochet hook

Abbreviations

See page 114

SKIRT

Ch112(120:128), join with a sl st to form a ring, being careful not to twist the chain; this is the most difficult part of this project!

Round 1: Ch1, 1sc into same place (this is a bit tricky as it is where the chain joins; if you find it easier you can add an extra st to the base chain), 1sc into every ch to end of rnd, join with a sl st to first sc made, do not turn. (112(120:128) sts)

Round 2 (eyelet rnd): Ch1, 1sc into same place, 1sc into next st, *ch2, skip 1 st, 1sc into each of next 4 sts; rep from * around, finishing with 1 sc into each of last 4(3:1) sts, join with a sl st to first sc, do not turn.

Small size only

Round 3 (increase rnd): (This rnd starts in the middle of the back: work 1dc into every ch2 space or st.) Ch3 (counts as 1dc), work 1dc into each of next 23 dc or ch 2 spaces, 2dc into next st, 1dc into each of next 6 sts, 2dc into next st, 1dc in each of next 49 sts, 2dc into next st, 1dc into each of next 6 dc, 2dc into next st, 1dc into each of next 23 sts, join rnd with a sl st to top of ch3, do not turn. (116 sts)

Check fit

Round 3 is the start of the waistband so it is worth checking to see if you can get it over your hips! Though it will loosen up a bit, if it feels too tight either go up a size or try a larger hook.

Medium size only

Round 3 (increase rnd): (This rnd starts in the middle of the back: work 1dc into every ch2 space or st.) Ch3 (counts as 1dc), work 1dc into each of next 24 sts, 2dc into next st, 1dc into each of foll 8 sts, 2dc into next st, 1dc into each of next 51 sts, 2dc into next st, 1dc into each of next 8 sts, 2dc into next st, 1dc into each of foll 24 sts, join rnd with a sl st to top of ch3, do not turn. *(124 sts)*

Large size only

Round 3 (increase rnd): (This rnd starts in the middle of the back: work 1dc into every ch2 space or st.) Ch3 (counts as 1dc), work 1dc into each of next 25 sts, 2dc into next st, 1dc into each of next 10 sts, 2dc into foll st, 1dc into each of next 54 sts, 2dc into next st, 1dc into each of next 10 sts, 2dc into next st, 1dc into each of next 24 sts, join rnd with a sl st top of ch3, do not turn. *(132 sts)*

All sizes

Round 4: Ch3 (counts as 1dc), 1dc into every st to first dc of 2 dc increase, 2dc into first of these dc, 1dc into next dc and every st to next 2 dc increase, 1dc into first of these dc and 2dc into next one, 1dc into next dc and every st to next 2 dc increase, 2dc into first of these dc, 1dc into next dc and every st to final 2 dc increase, 1dc into first of these dc and 2dc into next dc, 1dc into next st and every st to end of rnd, join with a sl st to top of ch3, do not turn. *(120(128:136) sts)*

Rounds 5–6: Rep rnd 4, do not turn. *(128(136:144) sts)*
The waistband is finished. Round 6 is first rnd shown on chart (on page 17).

Round 7 (first lace rnd): Ch1, 1sc into same place, *ch3, skip 1 st (be careful not to skip two sts as they are quite difficult to see), 1sc into next st; rep from * finishing with ch3, join rnd with sl st to first sc.

Round 8: Sl st into next ch 3 space, ch1, 1sc into same space, ch3, 1sc into next ch 3 space, 4 dc into foll ch 3 space, *1sc into next ch 3 space, ch3, 1sc into next ch 3 space, ch3, 1sc into foll ch 3 space, 4dc into next ch 3 space; rep from * finishing in last ch 3 space with 1sc, ch1, 1dc into top of first sc made in this rnd.

Round 9: Ch1, 1sc into top of dc, ch3, 1sc into next ch 3 space, *(1dc, ch1) into each of next 3 dc, 1dc into 4th dc, 1sc into next ch 3 space, ch3, 1sc into next ch 3 space; rep from * to end of rnd, finishing with a sl st to top of first sc made.

Round 10: Sl st into next ch 3 space, ch1, 1sc into same place, *ch2, dc3tog in the ch1 space between the 1st and 2nd dc, ch1, (dc3tog, ch1) into next ch 1 space, dc3tog into next ch 1 space, ch2, 1sc into ch 3 space; rep from * finishing with ch2, sl st into first sc made.

Round 11: Sl st into the ch 2 space, ch1, 1sc into same space, *ch4, skip 1 dc3tog, 1sc into ch 1 space, ch4, skip next dc3tog, 1sc into next ch 1 space, ch4, skip final dc3tog, 1sc into ch 2 space, ch4, 1 sc into next ch 2 space; rep from * to end of rnd, finishing with 1sc into last ch 2 space, ch2, 1dc into first sc made.

Round 12: Ch1, 1sc into top of dc, ch4, 1sc into next ch 4 space, *5dc into next ch 4 space (this should be directly over first group of rnd 8), 1sc into next ch 4 space, ch4, 1sc into next ch 4 space, ch4, 1sc into foll ch 4 space; rep from * to end of rnd, finishing with 1sc into last ch 4 space, ch2, 1dc into first sc made.

Round 13: Ch1, 1sc into top of dc, ch4, 1sc into next ch 4 space, *(1dc, ch1) into each of next 4 dc, 1dc into final dc, 1sc into next ch 4 space, ch4, 1sc into next ch 4 space; rep from * to end of rnd, finishing with 1dc into last dc of group of 5 dc, sl st to first sc made.

Round 14: Sl st twice into next ch 4 space, ch1, 1sc into same space, ch2,*(dc3tog, ch1) into each of first three ch 1 spaces, dc3tog in fourth ch 1 space, ch2, 1sc into ch 4 space, ch2; rep from * finishing after final group of dc3tog with ch2, join with sl st to first sc made.

Round 15: Sl st into next ch 2 space, ch1, 1sc into same place, *ch4, skip first dc3tog, 1sc into next ch 1 space, ch4, skip two dc3tog, 1sc into next ch 1 space, ch4, skip final dc3tog, 1sc into ch 2 space, ch4, 1sc into next ch 2 space; rep from * finishing with 1sc in last ch 2 space, ch2, 1dc into first sc made.

Rounds 16–18: Rep rnds 12–14.

Round 19: Rep rnd 15. If this rnd feels a bit tight, you can replace all the ch4 with ch5.

Round 20: Ch1, 1sc into top of dc, ch5, 1sc into next ch space, *7dc into foll ch space, 1sc into next ch space, ch5, 1sc into next ch space, ch5, 1sc into next ch space; rep from * finishing with 1sc in last ch 2 space, ch2, 1dc into first sc made.

Round 21: Ch1, 1sc into top of dc, ch5, 1sc into next ch 5 space, *(1dc, ch1) into each of next 6 dc, 1dc in final dc, 1sc into next ch 5 space, ch5, 1sc into next ch 5 space; rep from * to end of rnd, after final dc join rnd with a sl st to first sc made.

Round 22: Sl st twice into next ch 5 space, ch1, 1sc into same place, ch2, *(dc3tog, ch1) into each of next five ch 1 spaces, dc3tog in last ch 1 space, ch2, 1sc into next ch 5 space, ch2; rep from * finishing with ch2, join rnd with a sl st to first sc made.

Round 23: Sl st into next ch 2 space, ch1, 1sc into same place, *ch6, skip two dc3tog, 1sc into next ch 1 space, ch6, skip two dc3tog, 1sc into next ch 1 space, ch6, skip final two dc3tog, 1sc into ch 2 space, ch6, 1sc into next ch 2 space; rep from * finishing with 1sc into last ch 2 space, ch3, 1dc into first sc made.

Rounds 24–26: Rep rnds 20–22.

Round 27: Rep rnd 23.

Round 28: Ch1, 1sc into same place, ch6, 1sc into next ch 6 space, *9dc into next ch 6 space, 1sc into next ch 6 space, ch6, 1sc into foll ch 6 space, ch6, 1sc into next ch 6 space; rep from * finishing with 1sc into last ch 6 space, ch3, 1dc into first sc made.

Round 29: Ch1, 1sc into top of dc, ch6, 1sc into next ch 6 space, *(1dc, ch1) into each of next 8dc, 1dc into last dc, 1sc into ch 6 space, ch6, 1sc into next ch 6 space; rep from * finishing after final dc with a sl st into first sc made.

Round 30: Sl st twice into next ch 6 space, ch1, 1sc into same space, ch2, *work (dc3tog, ch1) into each of next seven ch1 spaces, dc3tog in last ch 1 space, ch2, 1sc into next ch 6 space, ch2; rep from * finishing with ch2, sl st into first sc made.

Round 31: Sl st into next ch 2 space, ch1, 1sc into same place, *ch6, skip three dc3tog, 1sc into next ch 1 space, ch6, skip two dc3tog, 1sc into next ch 1 space, ch6, skip final three dc3tog, 1sc into ch 2 space, ch6, 1sc into next ch 2 space; rep from * finishing with 1sc into last ch 2 space, ch3, 1dc into first sc made.

Rep rnds 28–31 until skirt is required length, ending after rnd 29. I have worked some silver thread along with the pima cotton in the last full repeat to give it a bit of sparkle.

Final round (picot round): Sl st twice into next ch 6 space, ch1, 1sc into same space, ch2, *work (dc3tog, ch3, sl st into the top of dc3tog, ch1) into each of next seven ch1 spaces, (dc3tog, ch3, sl st into the top of dc3tog) in last ch 1 space, ch2, 1sc into next ch 6 space, ch2; rep from * finishing with ch2, sl st into first sc made.
Fasten off.

DRAWSTRING

Using pima cotton and sparkle yarn double, ch181, 1sc into 2nd ch from hook and into each ch to end, do not fasten off, *ch3, sl st into 3rd of ch 3, ch3, sl st into same place as first sl st; rep from * 3 times more to make a flower, join rnd with a sl st, fasten off.
Starting in the middle of the skirt front, thread the drawstring through the eyelets made on row 2. When you have woven it through, make another flower as above and stitch to the plain end.

TO MAKE UP

Weave in ends (see page 125).

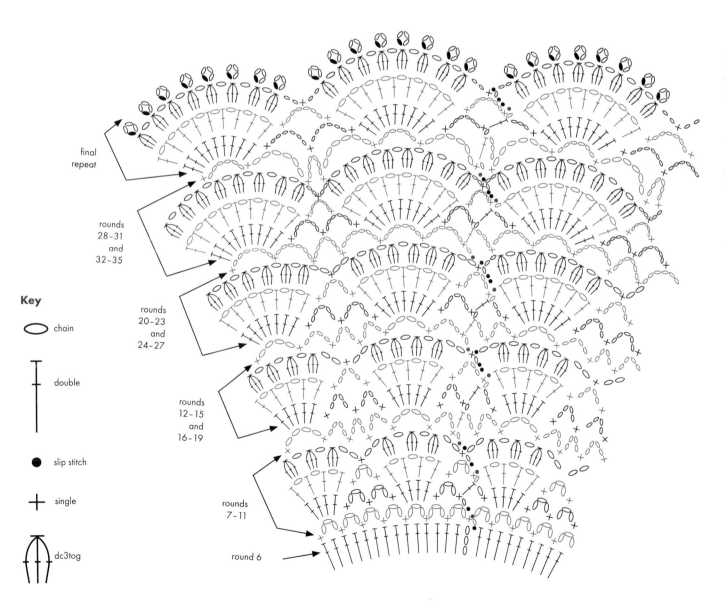

final
repeat

rounds
28–31
and
32–35

rounds
20–23
and
24–27

rounds
12–15
and
16–19

rounds
7–11

round 6

Key

⬭ chain

┬ double

● slip stitch

✕ single

⋀⋀ dc3tog

LACE *Sun Top*

This pretty, lacy top is a great way to try out pineapple lace, which is something every crocheter—in my personal opinion, of course—should try! Pineapple lace is traditionally viewed as rather old-fashioned and associated with doilies or antimacassars, but it is a beautiful stitch and can be used to wonderful effect in the modern world. This sun top looks great over a plain cami and is a beautiful addition to a summer wardrobe. I would count this as one of the slightly trickier projects in the book, but because of the relative complexity of the lace, I've kept the construction of the top very basic; shaping is achieved by making the pineapples larger. There is a chart as well as the written pattern to help you work the lace.

Yarn

Cascade Ultra Pima (100% pima cotton) sport-weight (double knitting) yarn, 3½oz (100g), 220yd (200m) skeins
3(4:4:5) skeins in Buttercup 3748

Hook and equipment

US E/4 (3.5mm) crochet hook
Large tapestry needle

Size

To fit: XS(S:M:L)
Finished measurements
Chest: 26(33½:41:48½)in (66(85:104:123)cm)
Length (excluding straps): 17(17:17:17)in (43(43:43:43)cm)

Gauge

One small pineapple motif (not including chains) measures 2in (5cm) long by 1½in (4cm) wide at widest point

Abbreviations

See page 114

BACK AND FRONT

(Make 2; worked from the top down)
Ch66(82:98:114) loosely.
Row 1: 1sc into 2nd ch from hook and into every ch to end, turn. (65(81:97:113) sts)
Row 2: Ch1, 1sc into same place, 1sc into every st to end, turn.
Row 3 (first row shown on chart): Rep row 2.
Row 4 (lace pattern): Ch1, 1sc into same place, ch3, skip 1 st, 1sc into next st, ch3, skip next st, 1sc into foll st, *ch5, skip 3 sts, 1sc into next st, ch5, skip 3 sts**, 1sc into foll st, [ch3, skip 1 st, 1sc into foll st] 4 times; rep from * to last 5 ch finishing at **, then 1sc, ch3, skip 1 st, 1sc into next st, ch3, skip next st, 1sc into last st, turn.
Row 5: Ch4, 1sc into first ch 3 space, ch3, 1sc into next ch 3 space, *ch5, (skip the ch 5 from row 4), 1dc into next sc, ch5, (skip next ch 5), 1sc into foll ch 3 space, ch3, 1sc into next ch 3 space**, ch3, 1sc into next ch 3 space, ch3, 1sc into final ch 3 space; rep from * to end of row, finishing at **, then ch1, 1dc into sc (at the start of row 4), turn.
Row 6: Ch1, 1sc into top of dc, ch3, 1sc into the ch 3 space, *ch5, (1dc, ch1, 1dc) into next dc, ch5, 1sc into next ch 3 space, ch3**, 1sc into foll ch 3 space, ch3, 1sc into last ch 3 space; rep from * to end of row, finishing at ** then working last sc into ch 4 space (turning ch from row 5), turn.
Row 7: Ch4, 1sc into first ch 3 space, *ch5, (1dc, ch1, 1dc, ch1, 1dc, ch1, 1dc, ch1, 1dc) into ch 1 space between 2 dc, ch5, 1sc into next ch 3 space, **ch3, 1sc into foll ch 3 space; rep from * finishing at ** then ch1, 1dc into last sc from row 6, turn.
Row 8: Ch8, skip ch 5, *(1sc, ch3) into each of next 4 dc, 1sc into final dc of group, ch5, 1dc into next ch 3 space, ch5; rep from * to end of row, finishing with ch5, 1dc into ch 4 space, turn.
Row 9: Ch8, *1sc into first ch 3 space of group, (ch3, 1sc) into each of next 3 ch spaces, ch5, skip ch 5, 1dc into the dc, ch5; rep from * to end of row, finishing with ch5, 1dc into ch 8 space, turn.

The rows above establish the pattern, see the chart for a guide for this part. After these rows the basic pattern remains the same except that the size of each pineapple increases by one row. If preferred, the same end result can be achieved by going up to a US F/5 (3.75mm) hook and repeating the pattern above.

Row 19: Ch4 (counts as 1dc, ch1), (1dc, ch1, 1dc, ch1, 1dc) into first dc, ch6, *1sc into first ch 3 space, ch3, 1sc into next ch 3 space, ch6, (1dc, ch1, 1dc, ch1, 1dc, ch1, 1dc, ch1, 1dc, ch1, 1dc) into ch 1 space between dc, ch6; rep from * to end of row, finishing with ch6, (1dc, ch1, 1dc, ch1, 1dc, ch1, 1dc) into top of ch 3, turn.

Row 20: Ch1, (1sc into dc, ch3) into each of next 3 dc, 1 sc into next dc, *ch6, 1dc into ch 3 space, ch6, (1sc, ch3) into each of next 5 dc, 1sc into final dc of group; rep from * to end of row, finishing with 1dc into last ch 3 space, ch6, 1sc into next dc, ch3, 1sc into foll dc, ch3, 1sc into next dc, ch3, 1sc into the ch 4 space, turn.

Row 21: Ch4, 1sc into first ch 3 space, (ch3, 1sc) into each of next two ch 3 spaces, * ch6, (skip the ch 6 space), 1dc into next dc, ch6, (skip next ch 6), (1sc, ch3) into each of next 4 ch 3 spaces, 1sc into final ch 3 space of group; rep from * to end of row, finishing after final ch 6 with 1sc into next ch 3 space, ch3, 1sc into next ch 3 space, ch3, 1sc into final ch 3 space, ch2, 1dc into the sc, turn.

Row 22: Ch1, 1sc into first dc, ch3, 1sc into next ch 3 space, ch3, 1sc into foll ch 3 space, *ch6, 1dc into next dc, ch6, (1sc, ch3) into each of next two ch 3 spaces, 1sc into final ch 3 space; rep from * to end of row, finishing after final ch 6 with 1sc into next ch 3 space, ch3, 1sc into next ch 3 space, ch3, 1sc into the ch 4 space, turn.

Row 23: Ch4, (counts as 1 dc, ch 1), 1sc into first ch 3 space, ch3, sc into next ch 3 space, *ch6, (1dc, ch1, 1dc) into next dc, ch6, (1sc, ch3) into each of next two ch 3 spaces, 1sc into final ch 3 space; rep from * to end of row, finishing after final ch 6 with 1sc into next ch 3 space, ch3, 1sc into next ch 3 space, ch2, 1dc into final sc, turn.

Row 24: Ch4, 1sc into first ch 3 space, ch6, *(1dc, ch1, 1dc, ch1, 1dc, ch1, 1dc, ch1, 1dc) into ch1 space between next 2 dc, ch6, *1sc into first ch 3 space, ch3, 1sc into next ch 3 space, ch6; rep from * to end of row, finishing after final ch 6 with 1sc into final ch 3 space, ch1, 1dc into the ch 4 space, turn.

Row 25: Ch9, *(1sc, ch3) into each of next 5 dc, 1sc into final dc of group, ch6, 1dc into next ch 3 space, ch6; rep from * to end of row, finishing after final ch 6 with 1dc into ch 4 space, turn.

Row 10: Ch3, 1dc into same place, *ch5, (1sc, ch3) into each of next two ch 3 spaces, 1sc into final ch 3 space of group, ch5, skip ch 5, (1dc, ch1, 1dc) into the dc; rep from * to end of row, finishing with ch5, 2dc into 3rd ch of ch 8, turn.

Row 11: Ch4 (counts as 1dc, ch1), (1dc, ch1, 1dc) into first dc, ch5, *1sc into first ch 3 space, ch3, 1sc into next ch 3 space, ch5, (1dc, ch1, 1dc, ch1, 1dc, ch1, 1dc, ch1, 1dc) into ch 1 space between dc, ch5; rep from * to end of row, finishing with ch5, (1dc, ch1, 1dc, ch1, 1dc) into top of ch 3, turn.

Row 12: Ch1, (1sc into dc, ch3) into each of next two dc, 1 sc into next dc, *ch5, 1dc into the ch 3 space, ch5, (1sc, ch3) into each of next 4 dc, 1sc into final dc of group; rep from * to end of row, finishing with 1dc into last ch 3 space, ch5, 1sc into next dc, ch3, 1sc into foll dc, ch3, 1sc into the ch 4 space, turn.

Rows 13–18: Rep rows 5–10 once more.

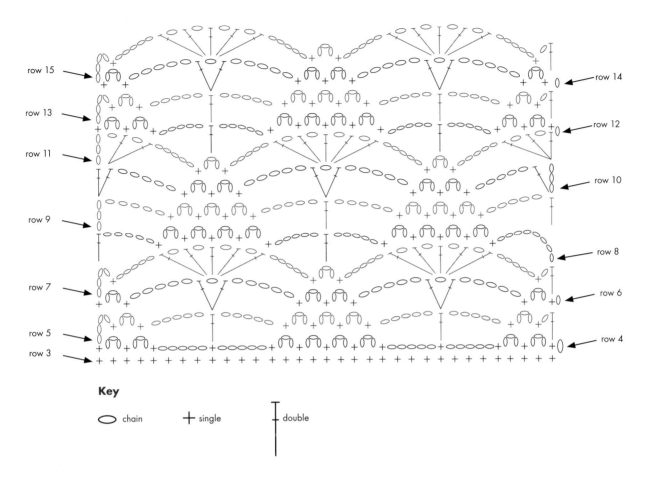

row 15
row 13
row 11
row 9
row 7
row 5
row 3

row 14
row 12
row 10
row 8
row 6
row 4

Key

⬭ chain   + single   ⊥ double

Row 26: Ch9, *(1sc, ch3) into each of next four ch 3 spaces, 1sc into final ch 3 space of group, ch6, 1dc into next dc, ch6; rep from * to end of row, finishing after first ch 6 with 1dc into ch 9 space, turn.

Row 27: Ch9, *(1sc, ch3) into each of next three ch 3 spaces, 1sc into final ch 3 space of group, ch6, 1dc into next dc, ch6; rep from * to end of row, finishing after first ch 6 with 1dc into ch 9 space, turn.

Row 28: Ch3, 1dc into same place, *ch6, (1sc, ch3) into each of next two ch 3 spaces, 1sc into final ch 3 space, **ch6, (1dc, ch1, 1dc) into next dc; rep from * to end of row, finishing at ** then ch6, 2dc into 3rd ch of ch 9, turn.

Row 29 onward: Rep rows 19–28 twice more, or until the top is the required length.

Final row: Rep row 19, fasten off.

TO MAKE UP

Weave in ends (see page 125).

Press before you sew up the top.

Place the front and back right sides together and seam up both sides; you can do this by either using sc or oversewing. Try the top on, work out how long you want the shoulder straps to be and then make a ch slightly longer than this for each strap (I have made a ch of 90). Work 3 rows of sc into the ch to complete each strap. Sew the straps into place.

CHUNKY *Cardigan*

Snuggly, chic, lightweight, and generally gorgeous, this cardigan will become invaluable as soon as you have finished it. The design is kept simple and rather like the Easy Crochet Sweater (see page 31), begins at the top, increasing at the raglan sleeves and then continuing down through the body. It has beautiful, slightly bell-shaped sleeves, and a proper collar that gives the cardigan a professional finish. This is really not at all difficult to crochet, and a great place to start if you are creating a garment for the first time. The sleeves are crocheted in the round, but this is very simple to do and shouldn't put you off.

Yarn

Mrs Moon Plump (80% superfine merino wool, 20% baby alpaca) super-bulky (super-chunky) yarn, 3½oz (100g), 76yd (70m) skeins

7(8:9) skeins in Cherry Pie

Hook and equipment

US O/17 (12mm) crochet hook
Large tapestry needle

Size

To fit: S(M:L)
Finished measurements
Chest: 37¾(41:44)in (96(104:112)cm)
Neck to underarm: 11(12½:13¾)in (28(31.5:35)cm)
Length (nape to hem): 22½in (57cm)
Sleeve (underarm seam):13½in (34cm)

Gauge

6 sts and 3.25 rows over 4in (10cm) using US O/17 (12mm) crochet hook

Abbreviations

See page 114

BODY

Ch36.

Row 1: 1dc into 4th ch from hook, 1dc into each of next 4 ch, (1dc, ch1, 1dc) into next ch, 1dc into each of next 3 ch, (1dc, ch1, 1dc) into next ch, 1dc into each of next 12 ch, (1dc, ch1, 1dc) into next ch, 1dc into each of next 3 ch, (1dc, ch1, 1dc) into next ch, 1dc into each of next 6 ch, turn. *(38 sts)*

The (1dc, ch1, 1dc) groups mark the four points of increase around the raglan sleeves.

Row 2: Ch3 (counts as 1 dc), 1dc into each of next 6 dc, (1dc, ch1, 1dc) into the ch 1 space, 1dc into each of next 5 dc, (1dc, ch1, 1dc) into next ch 1 space, 1dc into each of next 14 dc, (1dc, ch1, 1dc) into next ch 1 space, 1dc into each of next 5 dc, (1dc, ch1, 1dc) into next ch 1 space, 1dc into each of next 7 sts (the 7th dc is into top of the tch), turn. *(46 sts)*

Rows 3–8: Work in patt as set, increasing 4 times in every row at the ch 1 space from the previous row, turn. *(94 sts)*

Sizes M(L)

Work 1(2) more rows in patt. *(102(110) sts)*

Sizing the cardigan

The beauty of this pattern is that you can try it on as you go, allowing you to get to the right point to separate out for the sleeves (if the size you are working does not fit!).

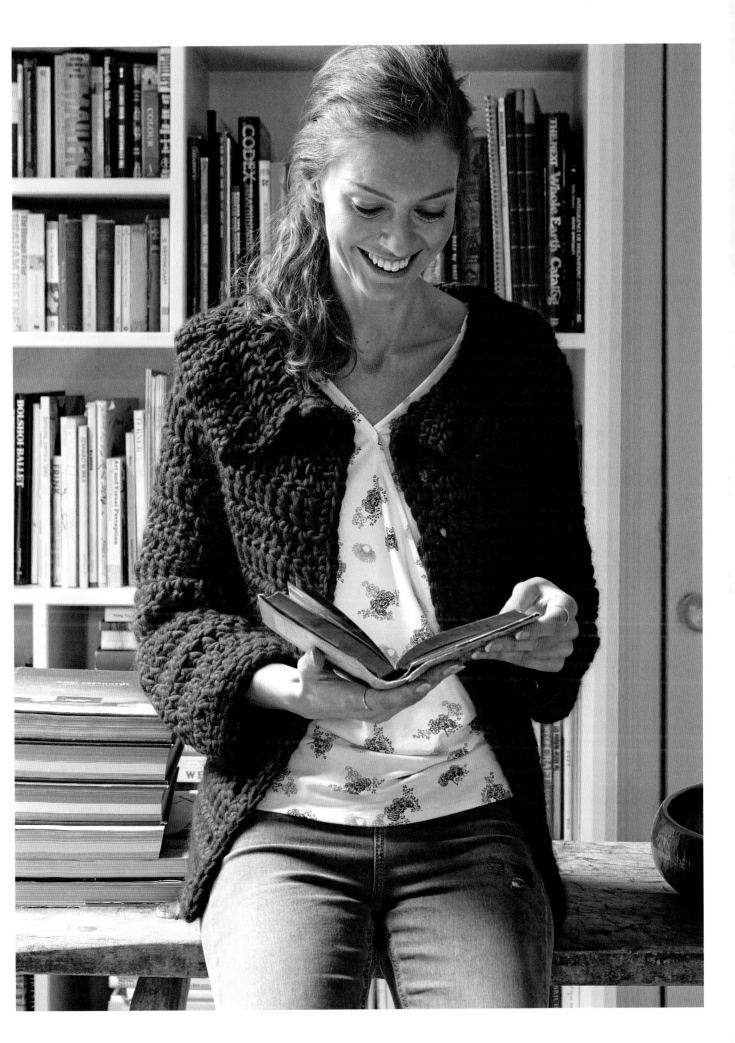

SHAPE ARMHOLES

Lay the body flat and tie a loop of contrast yarn through the ch 1 spaces on each side of both armholes; this makes it easier to see what you are doing. You are going to continue to work the body while leaving the two sets of sleeve sts unworked.

Row 1: Ch3 (counts as 1 dc), 1dc into each of next 13(14:15) sts, skip next ch 1 space, skip next 19(21:23) sts (these sts are for the first sleeve and will be returned to later), skip next ch 1 space, work 1dc in next dc (first underarm joined), 1dc into each of next 27(29:31) sts (along the back), skip next ch1 space, skip next 19(21:23) sts (second sleeve sts), skip next ch1 space, work 1dc in next dc (second underarm joined) 1dc into each of next 13(14:15) sts, working last dc into top of tch, turn. *(56(60:64) sts)*

Rows 2–11: Ch3 (counts as 1 dc), 1dc into every dc in previous row, working last st into top of the tch, fasten off. *(56(60:64) sts)* You can, of course, make your jacket longer by adding more rows before fastening off if you wish.

SLEEVE

I have decreased several times to bring the sleeves in; the great thing about working in the round in crochet is that you can try the garment on as you go, so check and see whether you want more or fewer decreases.

Round 1: With RS facing, join yarn to the first ch 1 underarm space at back of armhole, ch3 (counts as 1 dc), 1 dc into next 19(21:23) sts and into the last ch 1 space, join rnd with a sl st into top of ch 3, turn. *(21(23:25) sts)*

Round 2: Ch3 (counts as 1 dc), 1dc into every st, join rnd with a sl st into top of ch 3.
Rep rnd 2, 3 more times.

Round 6 (decrease): Ch3 (counts as 1 dc), dc2tog, 1dc into every st to end of rnd, join rnd with a sl st into top of ch 3, turn.

Round 7: Rep rnd 2.

Round 8: Rep rnd 6.

Rounds 9–10: Rep rnd 2.

Round 11: Ch1, 1sc into same place, 1sc into each st to end, join rnd with a sl st into top of first sc, fasten off.

You will have quite a large gap in the underarm because the stitches are quite high. When you have finished you can sew this up.

Rep for second sleeve.

COLLAR

Row 1: With RS facing, join the yarn to corner of right front neck of the cardigan, 1sc into each ch along foundation chain to left front neck corner, turn. *(34 sts)*

Row 2: Ch3 (counts as 1 dc), 1dc into each of next 5 sts, (1dc, ch1, 1dc) into next st, 1dc into each of next 3 dc, (1dc, ch1, 1dc) into next st, 1dc into each of next 12 sts, (1dc, ch1, 1dc) into next st, 1dc into each of next 3 sts, (1dc, ch1, 1dc) into next st, 1dc into each of last 6 sts, turn.

Work as for body for two more rows, working 1 dc into each dc and (1dc, ch1, 1dc) into each ch 1 space, fasten off.

TRIM

Starting in the middle of the back edge of collar, ch1, 1sc into same place, work 1 row of sc around entire edge of cardigan (as a general rule work 2sc into the side of each dc and work 3sc in every corner space): around the collar, down one front edge, around the bottom edge, up the other front edge, and around the other edge of collar to first sc, sl st to top of first sc to join, fasten off.

TO MAKE UP

Weave in ends (see page 125).

SPARKLY *Shrug*

This is so pretty! A shrug is a lovely cover-up for a special summer's evening, or adds a bit of glamour to a wintry night! And although the pattern is lacy, it is not at all difficult. The shrug is made in two rectangles sewn together, so that the lace pattern moves out from the center. You then simply seam up each end into a tube to make the arms. I have used a sparkly yarn, but you could also use the 100% cotton alternative below. Any sport-weight yarn would work; a silk mix would be particularly lovely, or a mercerized cotton.

Yarn

Scheepjes Twinkle DK (75% cotton, 25% polyester) sport-weight (double knitting) yarn, 1¾oz (50g), 142yd (130m) balls

7(8:8) balls in Black 903

Or: Cascade Ultra Pima (100% cotton) sport-weight (double knitting) yarn, 3½oz (100g), 219yd (200m) balls

4(5:4) balls in Night 3730

Hook and equipment

US F/5 or G/6 (4mm) crochet hook

Large tapestry needle

Size

To fit: S(M:L)

Finished measurements

Width before sewing for sleeves: 15(17:18¾)in (38(43:48)cm)

Length (along arms): 39½(41¾:44)in (100(106:112)cm)

Gauge

Each fan measures approx 2¼in (5.5cm) wide and 1¼in (3cm) high using US F/5 or G/6 (4mm) crochet hook

Abbreviations

PICOT = ch3, sl st into the 3rd ch from hook (if this looks too loose, then sl st into top of the double the picot is attached to by inserting hook from top to bottom and going through the two strands).

See also page 114

FIRST HALF OF SHRUG

Ch86(98:110) loosely.

Row 1: 1sc into the 2nd ch from hook, *ch5, skip 3 ch, 1sc into next ch; rep from * to end, finishing with 1sc into last ch, turn.

Row 2: Ch5 (counts as 1 dc, ch2), 1sc into ch 5 space, 8dc into next ch 5 space, *1sc into the foll ch 5 space, ch5, 1sc into next ch 5 space, 8 dc into next ch 5 space; rep from * to end of row, finishing with 1sc in final ch 5 space, ch2, 1dc into last sc, turn.

Row 3: Ch1 (does not count as st), 1sc into the first st, *(1dc, 1 picot) into the 1st dc of group of 8 dc, (1dc, 1 picot) into each of next 6 dc, 1dc into the final dc of group, 1sc into the ch 5 space; rep from * finishing with 1sc into the final ch 5 space, turn.

Row 4: Ch8 (counts as 1 dc, ch5), skip 2 picots, *1sc into 3rd picot, ch5, 1sc into 5th picot, ch5, skip 2 picots, 1dc into the sc, ch5, skip 2 picots; rep from * to end of row, finishing by working 1sc into 5th picot of last shell, ch5, skip last 2 picots, 1dc into last sc, turn.

Row 5: Ch5 (counts as 1 dc, ch2), 1sc into 1st ch 5 space, *8dc into next ch 5 space, 1sc into next ch 5 space, ch5, 1sc into next ch 5 space; rep from * to last ch 8 space, 1sc into this space, ch2, 1dc into the 3rd ch of the tch, turn.

Rep rows 3–5 until 17(18:19) reps completed, finishing with row 3.

SECOND HALF OF SHRUG

The second half of the shrug is worked from the base ch of the first half (the base ch will become the center back), as folls:

With RS of fabric facing, attach yarn to the 1st ch at RH edge and work as for first half of shrug, starting from row 1.

SLEEVES

The sleeves are made by seaming partway up each end of the shrug (which currently looks like a scarf). Sew or sc up from each end through 8 repeats, check fit, and sew more/less as necessary.

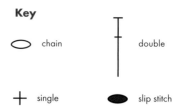

row 4 →

row 2 →

row 5

row 3

row 1

EDGING

Join yarn to top of center back seam, work 252(288:324) sc evenly around the neck opening, join with a sl st to the first sc made. This is to allow for 21(24:27) fans around the opening.

Round 1: Ch1, 1sc into same place, *ch5, skip 3 sts, 1sc into next st; rep from * to end of rnd, join with a sl st to 1st sc made.

Round 2: Sl st into next ch 5 space, **ch3 (counts as 1 dc), work 7 more dc into same ch 5 space, *1 sc into next ch 5 space, ch5, 1sc into the foll ch 5 space, 8dc into next ch 5 space; rep from * to last two ch 5 spaces, 1sc into next ch 5 space, ch5, 1 sc into last ch 5 space, join rnd with a sl st to top of ch 3.

Round 3: Ch3 (counts as 1 dc), picot, (1dc, picot) into each of next 6 dc, 1dc into the final dc of group, *1sc into next ch 5 space, (1dc, picot) into each of next 7 dc, 1dc into final dc of group; rep from * finishing with 1sc into last ch5 space, join rnd with a sl st to top of ch 3, fasten off.

Round 4: Rejoin yarn to last ch 5 space of rnd 3 (this is where you need to start this rnd), ch8 (counts as 1 dc, ch5), skip first 2 picots, 1sc into 3rd picot, ch5, 1sc into 5th picot, ch5, skip final two picots, *1dc into next sc, (1dc, picot) into each of next 7 dc, 1dc into last dc; rep from * to end of rnd, join with a sl st to 3rd ch of ch 8, fasten off.

Round 5: Skip next ch 5, rejoin yarn in foll ch 5 space (this should lie directly above last fan); rep rnd 2 from **.
Rep row 4 once more, fasten off.

TO MAKE UP

Weave in ends (see page 125).

Key

⬭ chain

━ double

+ single

⬬ slip stitch

TANK *Top*

Tank tops are so useful and versatile, and can get away with being made in all sorts of colors! I've always wanted to create a crochet tank top that is reminiscent of the traditional knitted Fair Isle versions, and I think I've managed it here! If you have never crocheted an actual garment before then this is a good place to start. The rib is very easy to work and the color patterning is basically granny stripes; it's a very simple design with no tricky shaping.

Yarn

Mrs Moon Plump DK (80% superfine merino wool, 20% baby alpaca) light-worsted-weight (double knitting) yarn, 1¾oz (50g), 125yd (115m) skeins

1(2:2:2) skeins in Gooseberry Fool (A)
1(1:2:2) skeins in Sugared Almond (B)
1(1:2:2) skeins in Pistachio Ice Cream (C)
1(1:2:2) skeins in Peppermint Cream (D)

If you want to make a plain colored tank top you will need: 4(5:5:6) skeins in color of your choice

Hooks and equipment

US G/6 or H/8 (4.5mm) and US H/8 or I/9 (5mm) crochet hooks
Large tapestry needle

Size

To fit: XS(S:M:L)
Finished measurements
Length (nape to hem, unstretched): 21(22¼:23¼:24½)in (53(56:59:62)cm)
Chest (unstretched): 27½(31½:35½:39½)in (70(80:90:100)cm)
This garment is designed to be fitted and will stretch

Gauge

4 x 3dc groups + 1 ch space and 8 rows over 4in (10cm) using US H/8 or I/9 (5mm) crochet hook

Abbreviations

See page 114

BACK

Using US G/6 or H/8 (4.5mm) hook and A, ch56(64:72:80) loosely.

Row 1: Work 2dc into 4th ch from hook, ch1, skip 3 ch, *3dc into next ch, ch1, skip 3 ch; rep from * to end of row, working 3dc into last ch, turn. *(14(16:18:20) 3dc groups)*

Row 2: Using B, ch4 (counts as 1 dc and 1 ch), 3dc into first ch 1 space, *ch1, 3dc into next ch 1 space; rep from * to end of row, finishing with 1 group of 3dc into last ch 1 space, ch1, 1dc into top of ch 3, turn. *(13(15:17:19) 3dc groups)*

Row 3: Using C, ch3 (counts as 1dc), 2dc into first ch 1 space, *ch1, 3dc into next ch 1 space; rep from * to end of row, finishing with 3dc into last ch 4 space, turn. *(14(16:18:20) 3dc groups)*

Work next row in D and keeping color stripe patt as set (1 row in each of A, B, C, D in turn), rep rows 2–3 until there are 11 rows in total, then change to US H/8 or I/9 (5mm) hook.
Cont in patt until there are 19 rows in total, turn.**
If you want your tank top to be longer, add more rows here, but you must finish with an odd number of rows.

SHAPE ARMHOLES
XS and S sizes only

Row 20: Without changing color, *1 sl st into each of next 3dc, 1 sl st into next ch 1 space; rep from * once more, change to next color in stripe patt, ch3 (counts as 1 dc), 2 dc into same ch 1 space; cont in patt until 11(13) groups of 3 dc have been worked, turn.

A perfect fit

I've deliberately made this tank top to finish at the waist and be very fitted. If you want to lengthen it I've noted in the pattern where you can do this, but bear in mind that you may need more yarn.

Checking your gauge

I am quite a loose crocheter, so I would really recommend you double-check your gauge before you get to the armholes! If you find that you are much tighter, try using a larger hook size or you could consider going up a size.

M and L sizes only

Row 20: Without changing color, *1 sl st into each of next 3dc, 1 sl st into next ch 1 space; rep from * twice more, change to next color in stripe patt, ch3 (counts as 1 dc), 2 dc into same ch 1 space; cont in patt until 13(15) groups of 3 dc have been worked, turn.

All sizes

Note: Continue to maintain color stripe patt as set.

Row 21: Ch4 (counts as 1 dc and 1 ch), 3 dc into first ch 1 space, cont in patt to end of row, finishing with 3dc into last ch 1 space, ch1, 1dc into top of ch 3, turn.

Cont in patt until 13(15:17:19) complete rows have been worked from start of armhole.

Fasten off.

FRONT

Using US G/6 or H/8 (4.5mm) hook and A, ch56(64:72:80) loosely.

Work as for Back to **. If you have made the back longer, then add the same number of extra rows here too.

Left-hand armhole

XS and S sizes only

Row 20 (RS): Without changing color, *1 sl st into each of next 3dc, 1 sl st into next ch 1 space; rep from * once more, change to next color in stripe patt, ch3 (counts as 1 dc), 2 dc into same ch 1 space, **ch1, 3dc into next ch 1 space; rep from ** once more (3 groups of 3 dc), turn.

M and L sizes only

Row 20: Without changing color, *1 sl st into each of next 3dc, 1 sl st into next ch 1 space; rep from * twice more, change to next color in stripe patt, ch3 (counts as 1 dc), 2 more dc into same ch 1 space, **ch1, 3dc into next ch 1 space; rep from ** once more (3 groups of 3 dc), turn.

All sizes

Row 21: Ch4 (counts as 1 dc and 1 ch), 3dc into ch 1 space, ch1, 3dc into next ch 1 space, ch1, 1dc into top of ch 3, turn.

Row 22: Ch3 (counts as 1 dc), 2dc into ch 1 space, ch1, 3dc into next ch 1 space, ch1, 3dc into ch 4 space, turn.

Rep rows 21–22 until 13(15:17:19) rows have been worked from start of armhole.

Fasten off.

RIGHT-HAND ARMHOLE

Row 20: With RS facing, starting at bottom left of left-hand armhole, skip 6(8:8:10) groups of 3dc on row 19, join yarn into next ch 1 space, ch3 (counts as 1 dc), 2dc into same ch 1 space, ch1, 3dc into next ch 1 space, ch1, 3dc into next ch 1 space, (3 groups of 3 dc), turn.

Row 21: Ch4 (counts as 1 dc and 1 ch), 3dc into ch 1 space, ch1, 3dc into next ch 1 space, ch1, 1dc into top of ch 3, turn.

Row 22: Ch3 (counts as 1 dc), 2dc into ch 1 space, ch1, 3dc into next ch 1 space, ch1, 3dc into ch 4 space, turn.

Rep rows 21–22 until 13(15:17:19) rows have been worked from start of armhole.

Fasten off.

TO MAKE UP

With RS together, sew or crochet up the shoulder seam and then each side seam. I prefer to seam with sc as I find it faster and easier to pull back when I go wrong (also, I am dreadful at sewing).

CROCHET RIB

Using A and US G/6 or H/8 (4.5mm) hook and with RS facing, join the yarn to the bottom LH side corner.

Ch1, 1sc into same space, 1sc into next st and into every st around bottom edge, join with a sl st to first sc (you will be working into the base chain).

Turn work sideways, ch16, sc into 2nd chain from hook and into every ch back to the garment, sl st into each of next two edge sc of the tank top, turn.

*Skip the two edge sl sts and work 1sc into BLO of every sc along the rib section (15 sts), turn.

Ch1, 1sc into BLO of every st back along the rib section to the garment, sl st into each of next two edge sc of the tank top, turn.

Rep from * around bottom edge of tank top. When you reach the end, fasten off. Use the large tapestry needle to join the two ends of the rib by sewing together through the BLO of both ends of the rib.

ARMHOLE TRIM

Using B and US G/6 or H/8 (4.5mm) hook and with RS facing, join yarn to underarm seam.

Work 1sc into every dc and 1 sc into every ch 1 space, working 2sctog around the corner, cont working evenly around the armhole, working 2sctog around the bottom corner.

As a general rule, when working along the sides of dc, work 2sc into each dc.

NECK TRIM

Work as for the armholes, starting at the middle of the back and remembering to work 2sctog into each of the 4 corners.

Fasten off.

Weave in ends (see page 125).

EASY CROCHET *Sweater*

I love a sloppy sweater that can be thrown over anything if it gets a bit chilly, but is still lovely and light, and looks great. This is one such item; it is so light-weight, but incredibly snuggly, and happens to look rather fabulous! The open-ness of the stitches gives it a slightly retro punk-rock feel, which is great too! This sweater is crocheted in the round, which means that there are no seams to sew up at the end (and that is surely always a good thing?!). Crocheting in the round is very simple and nowhere near as complicated as knitting in the round can sometimes seem, so even if you are a novice crocheter, I would thoroughly recommend giving this sweater a go!

Yarn

Mrs Moon Plump (80% superfine merino wool, 20% baby alpaca) super-bulky (super-chunky) yarn, 3½oz (100g), 76yd (70m) skeins

7(7:8) skeins in Sugared Almond

Hook and equipment

US O/17 (12mm) crochet hook

Large tapestry needle

Size

To fit: S(M:L)

Finished measurements

Chest: 35½(38:40½)in (90(96:102)cm)

Length (nape to hem): 22½(22½:22½)in (57(57:57)cm)

Sleeve (underarm seam): 13¾(15:16¼)in (35(38:41)cm)

Gauge

6 sts and 3.5 rows over 4in (10cm) using US O/17 (12mm) crochet hook

Abbreviations

See page 114

BODY

Ch32 loosely, join with a sl st to form a ring, being careful not to twist the chain. Make sure this loop fits over your head, it will loosen up!

Round 1: Ch4 (counts as 1 dc and 1 ch), 1dc into same space, 1dc into each of next 3 ch, (1dc, ch1, 1dc) in next ch, 1dc into each of next 11 dc, (1dc, ch1, 1dc) into next ch, 1dc into each of next 3 ch, (1dc, ch1, 1dc) into next ch, 1dc into each of next 11 dc, join rnd with a sl st to 3rd ch of ch 4, do not turn. *(36 sts)*

Note: The (1dc, ch1, 1dc) sets the points for the increases for the raglan sleeves. For orientation, the longer sections are the front/back and the shorter are the two sleeves.

Round 2: Sl st into ch 1 space, ch4 (counts as 1 dc and 1 ch), 1dc into same ch 1 space, *1dc into each of next 5 dc, (1dc, ch1, 1dc) into next ch 1 space, 1dc into each of next 13 sts,* (1dc, ch1, 1dc) into ch 1 space; rep from * to * once more, join rnd with a sl st into 3rd ch of ch 4. *(44 sts)*

Round 2 sets patt, with 1dc in each st and sleeve increases (1dc, ch1, 1dc) in every ch 1 space.

Work as set in rnd 2 until 8(9:10) rnds have been worked from foundation chain, join with a sl st to top of ch 3, do not fasten off yarn. *(92(100:108) sts)*

SHAPE ARMHOLES

I have increased here to give the sweater a boxy feel, this has been done by adding 4 sts, one either side of each armhole. Fold sweater along the "side seams" so you can clearly see the front and back and armholes.

Round 9(10:11): Sl st into 1 ch space, skip 19 dc and 1 ch space and sl st in dc on other side of armhole (you have now joined the 2 sides), ch3 (counts as 1 dc), 1dc into same st, 1dc into each st to next armhole, work 2dc into st before armhole, skip the two 1 ch spaces and 19(21:23) sts, 2dc into next st to make 2nd armhole (to secure this armhole tie a scrap of yarn through the bottom of the 2 dc either side of armhole; don't worry about the rather large hole in each underarm, you can

seam this once you have finished the sweater), 1dc into each st to end of rnd, working last dc into top of ch 3 from previous rnd, join with a sl st to top of ch 3.

Round 10(11:12): Ch3 (counts as 1dc), 1dc into next st and into every st to end of rnd, working 2 dc into last st of rnd, join with a sl st to top of ch 3. *(58(62:66) sts)*

Rep rnd 10(11:12) without increasing in last st until sweater is required length; I have worked a total of 19 rounds from the foundation chain for the smallest size.

Final round: Ch1, 1sc into same space, 1sc into next st and into every st to end of rnd, join with a sl st to first sc, fasten off.

SLEEVES

(Make 2)

Round 1: Turn sweater upside down, join yarn to 2nd dc that remained unworked (from the (1dc, ch1, 1dc)), ch3 (counts as 1 dc) work 1dc into each of next 18(20:22) sts, join with a sl st to top of ch 3 (last dc should be on the unworked st of the other (1dc, ch1, 1dc)). *(19(21:23) sts)*

Round 2: Ch3 (counts as 1dc), 1dc into next st and into every st to end of rnd, join with a sl st to top of ch 3. *(19(21:23) sts)*

Rounds 3–5: Rep rnd 2.

Round 6 (decrease): Ch3 (counts as 1dc), dc2tog, 1dc into next st and every st to end of rnd, join with a sl st to top of ch 3. *(18(20:22) sts)*

Round 7: Rep rnd 2.

Round 8 (decrease): Rep rnd 6. *(17(19:21) sts)*

Round 9: Rep rnd 2.

Round 10 (decrease): Rep rnd 6. *(16(18:20) sts)*

Round 11: Rep rnd 2.

At this stage try on sweater and if needed cont working rnds 6 and 2 until sleeves are required length.

Last round: Ch1, 1sc into same space, 1sc into next st and into every st to end of rnd, join with a sl st to first sc, fasten off.

NECK EDGING

Join yarn to the center back, ch1, 1sc into same space, work 1sc into each st to end of rnd, join with a sl st to top of first sc, fasten off. (You can, if you prefer, work another rnd of sc to make a slightly higher neckline.)

TO MAKE UP

Weave in ends (see page 125).

Sweater structure

You start from the neck and work down, increasing at the points where a raglan sleeve seam would be. Once you reach the point where the arms would start, you leave the sleeve stitches and carry on with just the body to the end of the sweater. Then it's just a case of finishing the sleeves off and you have a new wardrobe favorite!

CHAPTER 2

Scarves and Wraps

Whether you need something light and lacy for a summer evening party, or a warm and wooly number to snuggle into on a winter day, crochet is your best friend when it comes to making perfect scarves and wraps. And if you are a beginner to crochet, then start here, and don't be put off by the lace patterns; they are easier to work than you might think.

METALLIC *Luxury Cowl*

I think this is one of my favorite designs. The contrast of the squidgy Plump yarn and the fine metallic yarn creates a really beautiful effect, and it just oozes luxury! This is one of those designs that looks so tricky when in fact it just involves double crochet and chains and is easily a beginner project. You alternate the yarns—and crochet hooks—with each row and always work your doubles into spaces; it's so simple but so effective. And if you'd prefer not to use a metallic yarn, choose the 100% cotton Cascade Ultra Pima yarn below and go for a more subtle contrast that will still look amazing!

Yarn

Mrs Moon Plump (80% superfine merino wool, 20% baby alpaca) super-bulky (super-chunky) yarn, 3½oz (100g), 76yd (70m) skeins
  3 skeins in Fondant Fancy (A)

Scheepjes Twinkle DK (75% cotton, 25% polyester) sport-weight (double knitting) yarn, 1¾oz (50g), 142yd (130m) balls
  1 ball in Gold 941 (B)

Or: Cascade Ultra Pima (100% cotton) sport-weight (double knitting) yarn, 3½oz (100g), 219yd (200m) balls
  1 ball in Rich Gold 3866 (B)

Hooks and equipment

US N/15 (10mm) and US F/5 or G/6 (4mm) crochet hooks
Large tapestry needle

Size

60in (152cm) diameter and 9½in (24cm) deep

Gauge

7 dc sts and 3 rows over 4in (10cm) using A and US N/15 (10mm) crochet hook

Abbreviations

See page 114

COWL

Using A and US N/15 (10mm) hook, make a chain of 111, join with a sl st to form a ring, being careful not to twist the chain. You need to have a multiple of 3 sts for the next row, which 111 is, but I have not allowed for an extra st when I join the chain as I find it leaves a bit of a gap because I have quite a loose gauge. However, you may want to add an extra ch if you find the joined chain stitches too tight to work in to.

Round 1: Ch3 (counts as 1 dc), 1dc into next ch, and into every ch to end of rnd, join with a sl st to top of ch 3, fasten off.

Round 2: Using B and US F/5 or G/6 (4mm) hook, join yarn into space between any two dc, ch3 (counts as 1 dc), work 2dc into same space, *ch5, skip 3 dc, work 3dc into space between dc; rep from * to end of rnd, join with a sl st to top of ch 3, fasten off yarn and weave in ends.

Round 3: Using A and US N/15 (10mm) hook, join yarn into any ch 5 space, ch3 (counts as 1 dc), 2dc into same ch 5 space, 3 dc into next ch 5 space, and into every space to end of rnd. Join with a sl st to top of ch 3.

Rep rnds 2–3, weaving in ends of B as you go, until 7 rnds of A have been completed.

Next round: Using A and US N/15 (10mm) hook, ch1, 1sc into same st, and then into every st to end of rnd, join with a sl st to top of first sc, fasten off.

TO MAKE UP

Weave in ends of A (see page 125).

Weave as you go

Take the time to weave in the ends of the metallic yarn after each round. It's so slippery that it can unravel otherwise, and that is a tad annoying!

MANLY HOUNDSTOOTH *Scarf*

If you are looking for a really very simple project, here it is! Using only basic stitches, you can make this super-quick but totally lovely scarf, which is rather manly when worked in these colors, but you can obviously go to town with color combinations! As I do with all luxury yarns, I've tried to make sure that there is very little wastage from your two balls. To ensure that you have enough yarn, leave only very short tails, just long enough to weave in, when you switch colors.

Yarn

Valley Yarns Becket (50% alpaca, 50% wool) worsted-weight (Aran) yarn, 3½oz (100g), 141yd (129m) balls
    1 ball in Storm Cloud 25 (A)
    1 ball in Cornflower 26 (B)

Hook and equipment

US K/10½ (6.5mm) crochet hook
Large tapestry needle

Size

61½ x 4½in (156 x 11cm)

Gauge

9.5 sts and 9 rows over 4in (10cm) using US K/10½ (6.5mm) crochet hook, measured over sc/dc stitch pattern

Abbreviations

See page 114

SCARF

Using A, ch150 loosely. (The stitch pattern works with any multiple of 2, so it is easy to make the scarf longer or shorter—remember to purchase extra yarn if necessary.)
Row 1: 1sc into 4th ch from hook, *1dc into next ch, 1sc into foll ch; rep from * to end of row, finishing with 1sc, fasten off A, turn.
Row 2: Join in B, ch3 (counts as 1dc), skip st at base of ch 3, *1sc into next st, 1dc into foll st; rep from * to end of row (you should be working sc sts into dc sts and dc sts into sc sts), finish with 1sc into top of tch, fasten off B, turn.
Rep row 2, alternating between A and B. I worked 10 rows, finishing with a B row.

TO MAKE UP

Weave in ends (see page 125).

Starting the scarf

The scarf is worked lengthwise, so you need to be very careful when you make your foundation chain that it is really loose. If it's too tight, not only will the first row be a nightmare, but the scarf will also curve to one side. If you have a problem creating an even, loose chain, use a crochet hook a few sizes larger for this, then switch back to a US K/10½ (6.5mm) hook for the first row.

RIPPLE *Shawl*

This gorgeous bit of fluff and sparkle is perfect for the sophisticated woman that I like to think I could be if life had taken a different path! It is the kind of shawl that is timeless and can be pulled out again and again when you need something to cover your shoulders over a strappy evening gown. The pattern is a basic ripple stitch, but uses two really special yarns; the contrast between the shiny metallic and the sumptuous fluffiness produces a gorgeous effect. The pattern also includes a 100% cotton alternative for the metallic yarn which would give an equally beautiful finish. There is a chart as well as the pattern to help you work the stitch.

Yarn

Drops Kid Silk (25% silk, 75% mohair) fingering (lace-weight) yarn, ¾oz (25g), 229yd (210m) balls
 2 balls in Chalk 38 (A)

Rowan Anchor Artiste Metallic (80% viscose, 20% polyester) fingering (lace-weight) yarn, ¾oz (25g), 109yd (100m) balls
 2 balls in Gold 300 (B)

Or: Scheepjes Maxi Sweet Treat (100% cotton) fingering (lace-weight) yarn, ¾oz (25g), 153yd (140m) balls
 2 balls in Gold 154 (B)

Hook and equipment

US F/5 or G/6 (4mm) crochet hook
Large tapestry needle

Size

13 x 45in (33 x 114cm)

Gauge

1.5 pattern reps and 9 rows over 4in (10cm) using US F/5 or G/6 (4mm) crochet hook

Abbreviations

See page 114

SHAWL

Using A, ch213 loosely.

Row 1: 2dc into 4th ch from hook, *1dc into each of foll 3 ch, [dc3tog] twice (so worked over next 6 ch, this is the decrease at the bottom of the wave), 1dc into each of next 3 ch, 3dc into each of next 2 ch (this is the increase at the top of the wave); rep from * to end of row, finishing after final decrease with 1dc into each of next 3 ch and 3dc into final ch, turn.

Row 2: Ch3 (counts as 1 dc), 2dc into st at base of ch3, *1dc into each of foll 3 sts, [dc3tog] twice (this should fall directly above the decrease on the row below), 1dc into each of next 3 sts, 3dc into each of foll 2 sts; rep from * to end of row, finishing with 1dc into each of last 3 sts, 3dc into top of tch (the skipped sts at beg of row 1), turn, fasten off A.

Row 3: Join in B, ch3 (counts as 1 dc), 2dc into st at base of ch 3, *1dc into each of next 3 sts, [dc3tog] twice, 1dc into each of foll 3 sts, 3dc into each of foll 2 sts; rep from * to end of row, finishing with 1dc into each of last 3 sts and 3dc into top of tch, turn, fasten off B.

Rep row 3, working 3 rows of A followed by 1 row of B until 7 stripes of B have been worked in total, then work 2 rows of A, do not fasten off A.

Using the mohair yarn

It can be a bit tricky working with the mohair yarn, just in terms of being certain of where the stitches are, so you might want to practice the stitch pattern with a smoother yarn first, just so you know what it's supposed to look like before you add in the mohair complication!

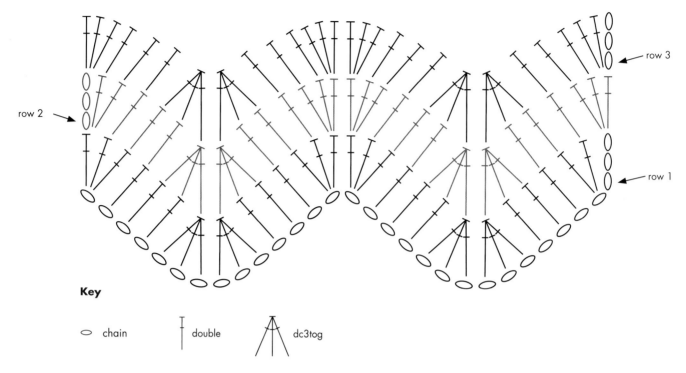

← row 3

row 2 →

← row 1

Key

⬭ chain   ⊺ double   ⅄ dc3tog

EDGING

Cont in A, work 1 row of sc neatly down LH edge of shawl (as a general rule work 2sc along the length of each dc), fasten off yarn. Rep along RH edge.

Join B at top of LH edge, ch1, 1sc into same st, 1sc into each of next 2 sts, *ch3, sl st into 3rd ch from hook (picot made), skip next st, 1 sc into each of foll 3 sts; rep from * to bottom of edge, fasten off. Rep along RH edge.

TO MAKE UP

Weave in ends (see page 125).

Using the metallic yarn

Weave in the ends of the metallic yarn as you go as it is very slippery, and securing it straight away will avoid any unraveling disasters.

WATERFALL *Scarf*

This beautiful scarf looks complicated to make, but actually is quite simple once you have set the pattern up. It is a four-row repeat that becomes very clear early on, so it is easy to see if you have made a mistake, and there are constant reference points to ensure that you don't go astray! The gorgeous tones of blues are reminiscent of gushing water, but don't let that put you off choosing different shades: rich yellows and oranges would be amazing, or how about four tones of green? The scarf is joined in the middle so that the pattern cascades down to the ends on both sides; this means that you don't have a flat edge at one end and a pretty edge at the other!

Yarn

Valley Yarns Northfield (70% merino wool, 20% alpaca, 10% silk) light-worsted-weight (double knitting) yarn, 1¾oz (50g), 124yd (113m) balls

2 balls in Stone Blue 24 (A)
1 ball in Tranquil Blue 27 (B)
2 balls in Light Grey LGRY (C)

Hook and equipment

US E/4 (3.5mm) crochet hook
Large tapestry needle

Size

59 x 11in (150 x 28cm)

Gauge

Each shell measures 2¾in (7cm) by 2in (5cm) using US E/4 (3.5mm) crochet hook

Abbreviations

See page 114

FIRST HALF OF SCARF

Using A, ch58.

Row 1: Work 1sc into 2nd ch from hook and into every ch to end of row, turn. *(57 sts)*

Row 2: Ch6, skip st at base of ch 6 and next sc, 1sc into next sc, *ch5, skip 2 sc, 1sc into next sc, ch5, skip 3 sc, 1sc into next sc, ch5, skip 2 sc, 1sc into next sc, ch5, skip 3 sc, 1sc into next sc; rep from * twice more, then rep again to last 2 sts, ch2, skip 1sc, 1dc into last sc, turn. *(17 loops)*

Row 3: Ch1, 1sc into first dc, ch5, 1sc into first ch 5 space, 7dc into next ch 5 space, *1sc into next ch 5 space, ch5, 1 sc into next ch 5 space, ch5, 1sc into next ch 5 space, 7dc into next ch 5 space; rep from * and after 4th set of 7dc groups finish with 1sc into next ch 5 space, ch5, 1sc into last ch 6 space, turn, fasten off.

Row 4: Join in B, ch5, 1sc into first ch 5 space, *1dc into next dc, (ch1, 1dc) into each of next 6 dc, 1 sc into next ch 5 space, ch5, 1sc into next ch 5 space; rep from * and after 4th set of dc groups finish with 1sc into next ch 5 space, ch2, 1dc into sc, turn, fasten off.

Row 5: Join in C, ch1, 1sc into dc, *(hdc3tog, ch3, sl st into top of hdc to make picot, ch2) into each of next 7 dc (do not work the final ch 2), 1sc into next ch 5 space; rep from * and after 4th set of dc groups finish with 1sc into last ch 5 space, turn, fasten off.

Row 6: Join in A, ch6, skip 2 picots, * 1 sc into ch 2 space (between picots 2 and 3), ch5, skip 1 picot, 1sc into next ch 2 space, ch5, 1sc into next ch 2 space, ch5, 1sc into next ch 2 space, ch5, skip 4 picots (2 picots from group you are working on and first 2 picots from next group); rep from * up to and including last 2 picots, ch2, 1tr into last sc, turn.

Rep rows 3–6, 14 times more.

row 6 →
row 5 ←
row 4 →
row 3 ←
row 2 →
row 1 ←

Key

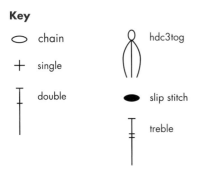

⬭ chain

＋ single

╪ double

🙂 hdc3tog

⬤ slip stitch

╪ treble

SECOND HALF OF SCARF

So that the pattern works down toward both ends of the scarf you need to work the second half from what will be the middle of the scarf (currently the base chain of the first side).

Turn the scarf to the wrong side (the cast-on tail should be at the opposite end to where you are about to start working) and work along the base chain as for patt row 2. Cont in patt as for first half until 15 reps are completed.

TO MAKE UP

Weave in ends (see page 125).

LARGE BOBBLE *Cross Double Scarf*

I love everything about this scarf: the tassels that balloon like mini pompoms, the color, the size, and the altogether bold statement that it makes! What's not to love? Crossing doubles is one of those techniques that looks very complicated and fancy, and in fact is so simple that you feel a little as though you're cheating by working it so easily. The stitch gives what could be quite a plain pattern a beautiful twist (quite literally), and is shown off to fabulous effect here. The quirky bobble fringe gives a great finish to the scarf, but is added on at the end, so if you'd rather leave it off, then that's no problem.

Yarn

Mrs Moon Plump (80% superfine merino wool, 20% baby alpaca) super-bulky (super-chunky) yarn, 3½oz (100g), 76yd (70m) skeins

7 skeins in Marmalade

Hook and equipment

US N/15 (10mm) crochet hook
Large tapestry needle

Size

70 x 12in (177 x 30cm) (excluding tassels)

Gauge

4 x cross doubles and 5 rows (2 cross double rows and 3 sc rows) over 4in (10cm) using US N/15 (10mm) crochet hook

Abbreviations

cdc : cross double = skip 1 st/ch, work 1dc, then work 1 dc into st/ch that was skipped, going back across first dc made.
See also page 114

SCARF

Ch28 loosely.

Row 1 (cdc row): Work 1dc into 5th ch from hook, then 1dc into 4th ch from hook, crossing back across first dc made (first cdc made), skip next ch and work 1dc into next ch, then work back across last dc into ch that was skipped (second cdc made); cont working cdc to last ch, 1dc into last ch, turn. *(12 cdc)*

Row 2 (sc row): Ch1 (does not count as st), 1sc into same st, 1sc into next st and into every st to end of row, working last sc into top of ch 3, turn. *(26 sc)*

Row 3 (cdc row): Ch3 (counts as 1dc), skip st at base of ch 3, *work 1cdc over foll 2 sts; rep from * to end of row, finishing with 1dc into last st, turn. *(12 cdc)*

Rep rows 2–3 until you have used up 6 skeins of yarn. Weigh the final skein, then work the bobble fringe on the starting end of the scarf, then weigh the skein again. The amount used is what is needed for the bobble fringe at the other end of the scarf, so wind off that amount. Then use the remainder of the skein to cont working rows 2–3, finishing with a row 2. Work bobble fringe along finishing end of scarf.

BOBBLE FRINGE

Attach yarn to a corner of starting edge, *ch8, dc3tog into 4th ch from hook, ch4, dc3tog into 4th ch from hook, sandwich the two groups together, and work a sl st through bottom of first dc3tog to secure (first bobble made), ch4, sl st into next 4 sts along on edge of scarf; rep from * along bottom edge of scarf. Do not worry too much if the spacing is not exactly even, but make sure the last bobble is made at the far corner: I made 7 bobbles at each end of the scarf.

TO MAKE UP

Weave in ends (see page 125).

OMBRÉ *Tassel Scarf*

This scarf is a very simple pattern made so beautiful by the stunning yarn. The yarn runs from gray to pink on one giant ball. Choose any graduated sock-weight (4ply) yarn and you will get a similar effect—the beauty of this is that no scarf will be the same as any other. If you prefer, use a yarn in a gorgeous and soft natural fiber such as 100% cotton or a silk-mix.

Yarn

Scheepjes Whirl (40% acrylic, 60% cotton) sock-weight (4-ply) yarn, 7¾oz (220g), 1094yd (1000m) balls
  1 ball in Watermelon Hell Raiser 784

Hook and equipment

US B/1 or C/2 (2.5mm) crochet hook
Tapestry needle

Size

50½ x 11½in (128 x 29cm) (excluding tassels)

Gauge

7 groups of 3 dc (including 6 x 1 ch spaces) and 2 complete pattern reps over 4in (10cm) using US B/1 or C/2 (2.5mm) crochet hook

Abbreviations

See page 114

SCARF

Ch79 loosely.

Row 1: 1dc into 4th ch from hook, 1 dc into each of next 2 ch, *ch1, skip 1 ch, 1dc into each of next 3 ch; rep from * to end of row, finishing last 5 chs with ch1, skip 1 ch, 1dc into each of last 4 chs, turn.

Row 2: Ch3 (counts as 1dc), skip st at base of ch 3, 1dc into next st, *ch1, skip 1 st, 1dc into next st, 1dc into ch 1 space, 1dc into foll st; rep from * to last 3 sts, ch1, skip 1 st, 1dc into last st, 1dc into top of ch 3, turn.

Row 3: Ch3 (counts as 1dc), skip st at base of ch 3, *1dc into next st, 1dc into ch 1 space, 1dc into foll st, ch1, skip 1 dc; rep from * to last 4 sts, finishing with 1dc into next dc, 1dc into ch 1 space, 1dc into last st and 1dc into top of ch 3, turn.

Row 4: Ch1 (does not count as st), 1sc into first dc, ch5, skip 3 dc, 1sc into ch 1 space, *ch5, skip 3 dc, 1sc into next ch 1 space; rep from * to end of row, finishing with 1sc into last ch 1 space, ch5, skip 3 dc, 1sc into top of ch 3, turn.

Row 5: Ch5, 1sc into first ch 5 space, *ch5, 1sc into next ch 5 space; rep from * to end of row, finishing with 1sc into last ch 5 space, ch2, 1dc into sc, turn.

Row 6: Ch1 (does not count as st), 1sc into first dc, ch3, 1sc into first ch 5 space, *ch3, 1sc into next ch 5 space; rep from * to end of row, finishing with 1sc into last ch 5 space, turn.

Row 7: Ch3 (counts as 1dc), 3dc into first ch 3 space, *ch1, 3dc into next ch 3 space; rep from * to end of row, finishing with 3dc into last ch 3 space, 1dc into sc, turn.

Rep rows 2–7 until scarf measures desired length, finishing with a row 3.

TO MAKE UP

Weave in ends (see page 125).
Space 17 tassels evenly along each end of the scarf, attaching them with a standard cow hitch knot (see page 124).

Making the tassels

If you want the tassels to match the color of the yarn at each end of the scarf, then wind off yarn for first set before you start, and the final set when you get toward the end of the ball. I have put the tassels at contrasting ends, but you can make yours harmonious with the crochet if you prefer. I have made 17 tassels for each end, using 30in (75cm) per tassel, that's 28¼yd (25.5m) in total.

CHAPTER 3
For the Home

Crochet is the perfect craft for making gorgeous items for your home. Large, flat items—such as blankets, throws, and rugs—show off the texture of crochet stitches beautifully, and allow for a lot of color work without making the finished result look too busy. And using a chunky yarn and large hook will make even the biggest project grow more quickly than you might think.

BIG *Bedrunner*

This bedrunner is such a beautiful piece of crochet, and very easy to make. The possibilities of size and color are endless, and you can really have fun creating something completely original for your own room. The pattern is just a mix of singles and doubles so it really is suitable for a total beginner. Also, using such a chunky yarn means that it grows very quickly, which is never a bad thing in my book!

Yarn

Mrs Moon Plump (80% superfine merino wool, 20% baby alpaca) super-bulky (super-chunky) yarn, 3½oz (100g), 76yd (70m) skeins

  2 skeins in Pavlova (A)
  2 skeins in Fondant Fancy (B)
  2 skeins in Pistachio Ice Cream (C)
  2 skeins in Peppermint Cream (D)
  2 skeins in Gooseberry Fool (E)
  2 skeins in Sugared Almond (F)

Hook and equipment

US N/15 (10mm) crochet hook
Large tapestry needle

Size

58 x 22¾in (147 x 58cm)

Gauge

6.5 sts and 6.5 rows over 4in (10cm) using US N/15 (10mm) crochet hook

Abbreviations

See page 114

BEDSPREAD

Using A, ch98.
Row 1: 1sc into 4th ch from hook, *1dc into next ch, 1sc into foll ch; rep from * to end of row, finishing with 1sc into last ch, turn, fasten off.
Row 2: Ch3 (counts as 1 dc), *1sc into next st, 1dc into foll st; rep from * to end of row, finishing with 1sc into top of tch, turn, fasten off.
Rep row 2, noting that you should be alternating sc and dc on each row, and every sc should work onto a dc from the row below, and changing color as folls:
Row 3: B.
Row 4: C.
Row 5: D.
Row 6: E.
Row 7: F.
Row 8: F.
Row 9: E.
Row 10: D.
Row 11: C.
Row 12: B.
Row 13: A.
Row 14: A.
Rep rows 3–14 stripe patt twice more.

TO MAKE UP

Weave in ends (see page 125), or see below.

Changing the size

If you want to make the bedrunner larger or smaller, the pattern repeat is simply a multiple of two, and the length of the chain will be the final width. You can weave in the ends, but for this runner I have left them as a fringe; it's not just laziness, it looks great!

Working the foundation chain

One tip that will make a big difference is to make the foundation chain very loose. This is always a good idea in crochet, but particularly here if you are a total beginner; this is the one thing that could spoil the finish. If you find it difficult to create a loose chain, go up a hook size for this first bit, switching back to a US N/15 (10mm) hook for the first row.

THREE *Scatter Pillows*

These scatter pillows are a great place to start if you are new to crochet. They are great projects for trying out different types of granny square and practising singles and doubles. The fun borders are all easy to create, too, and give the pillows a really lovely finish.The yarn specified is enough for all three pillows, but you can obviously just make one if you prefer. If you have a bigger pillow pad, why not make one of the granny square pillow covers and just keep going round and round, or making extra squares, until it fits! The patterns are just for the front of the pillows; I find it's better to back them with fabric. This helps them keep their shape and it also seems such a waste to crochet something that no one will ever see! You could however, mix and match these patterns for fronts and backs, which will mean you can get a change of look in your room with a flip of a pillow!

Yarn

Spud & Chloe Sweater (55% superwash wool, 45% organic cotton) worsted-weight (Aran) yarn, 3½oz (100g), 160yd (146m) skeins

3 skeins in Ice Cream 7500 (A)

1 skein in Watermelon 7512 (B)

1 skein in Pollen 7508 (C)

1 skein in Firefly 7505 (D)

Hook and equipment

US G/6 or H/8 (4.5mm) crochet hook

Large tapestry needle

3 x 16in (40cm) square pillow pads or pillows with covers

Size

16in (40cm) square (excluding borders)

Gauge

13 dc sts and 6.5 rows over 4in (10cm) using US G/6 or H/8 (4.5mm) crochet hook

Abbreviations

See page 114

FLOWER PILLOW

Using C, ch6, join with a sl st to form a ring.

Round 1: Ch6 (counts a 1dc and ch3), *1dc into ring, ch3; rep from * 6 more times, join with sl st to 3rd ch of ch 6, fasten off C. *(8 spokes and 8 spaces)*

Round 2: Join A to any ch 3 space, (1sc, ch2, 3dc, ch2, 1sc) into same space, *(1sc, ch2, 3dc, ch2, 1sc) into next ch 3 space; rep from * 6 times and do not join rnd at the end. *(8 sets of petals)*

Round 3: *Ch5, now work behind the petals from the previous row, skip 1 petal, 1sc into next dc of previous rnd (rnd 1, in between the petals); rep from * to end of rnd, do not join rnd at the end. *(8 x ch 5 loops)*

Round 4: *(1sc, ch2, 5dc, ch2, 1sc) into next ch 5 loop; rep from * to end of rnd, do not join rnd at the end. *(8 petals)*

Round 5: *Ch7, now work behind the petals from the previous row, 1sc into next sc of previous rnd (rnd 3); rep from * to end of rnd, do not join rnd at the end. *(8 x ch 7 loops)*

Round 6: *(1sc, ch2, 7dc, ch2, 1sc) into next ch 7 loop; rep from * to end of rnd, join with sl st to first sc, fasten off A. *(Flower is complete)*

The 'granny square' part of the pillow cover is worked directly onto the flower from rnd 7 onward.

Round 7: Join B to any sc on rnd 5, working behind the petals, ch 3 (counts as 1dc), 2dc into same space, ch1, *(3dc, ch2, 3dc) into next sc of rnd 5 to make a corner, ch1, **3dc into next sc, ch1; rep from * twice then from * to ** only once more, join with a sl st to top of ch 3. *(4 corners and 4 sides).*

Round 8: Sl st into next 2 dc and into ch 1 space, ch3 (counts as 1dc), 2dc into same space, ch1, *(3dc, ch2, 3dc) into corner space, ch1, 3dc into next space, ch1, 3dc into next space, ch1; rep from * to end of rnd, join with a sl st to top of ch 3.

Cont working as set in rnd 8 for 10 more rnds, working 3dc into every ch1 side space, working 1ch in between each 3dc, and (3dc, ch2, 3dc) into every corner space. Work rnds 9 and 10 in B, rnds 11 and 15 in A, rnds 12, 13, and 14 in D, and rnds 16, 17, and 18 in C.

When joining a new color, always join in a ch 1 space starting as folls: ch3 (counts as 1dc), 2dc into same ch space.

Round 19: Join A to any side st from rnd 19, ch1, 1 sc into same st, 1sc into every st and 1sc into every ch 1 space, working 2sc into every ch 2 corner space, join rnd with a sl st to top of first sc, do not fasten off yarn.

BOBBLE EDGING

Round 20: *Ch5, work hdc3tog into 3rd ch from hook, secure yarn by yoh, ch2, hdc3tog into 3rd ch from hook (top of previous hdc3tog), sandwich the two groups together and secure with a sl st through the bottom of first group to form a bobble, ch3, skip 3 sc along the edge of the pillow, join to edge with a sl st in foll st; rep from * around edge of pillow cover, skipping just 1 st rather than 3 sts at each corner, join rnd with a sl st, fasten off.

STRIPY PILLOW

Using D, ch50.

Row 1: 1 sc into 4th ch from hook, *1dc into next ch, 1sc into foll ch; rep from * to end of chain, finishing with 1sc into last ch, fasten off D.

Row 2: Join in B, ch3 (counts as 1dc), skip st at base of ch 3, *1sc into next st, 1dc into foll st; rep from * to end of row, finishing with 1sc into top of ch 3, fasten off B.

Row 3: Join A; rep row 2.

Rep row 2 for a further 41 rows, changing color on each row in order as set: D, B, A.

JOINING SQUARES

Lay the squares out flat in the order that you want them, or follow the photograph. Crochet the squares together (see page 123) to make horizontal strips, then join those to complete the pillow. With wrong sides facing and using A, work sl sts through both loops of each square. If you prefer you can sew the squares together, but I find it much easier to crochet them and the ridge between each square is a nice feature.

BORDER

Round 1: Join A to any ch 2 corner space, 3sc into same space, 1sc into every st and 1sc into every ch 1 space around pillow, working 3sc into every corner space. It is a bit tricky working over the seams; I have worked 1sc into each of the ch 2 spaces either side of a seam, but the main thing is to try and keep the sts as even as possible, join with a sl st to first sc made, do not fasten off.
Round 2: Ch3 (counts as 1dc), work 3dc into next st (corner turned), 1dc into next st, and into every st around pillow, working 3dc into every corner st (middle sc of 3 sc), join rnd with a sl st to top of ch 3, do not fasten off.
Round 3 (picot round): Ch1, 1sc into same st, *ch3, sl st into 3rd ch from hook, skip next st, 1sc into each of next 3 sts; rep from * around pillow, join with a sl st to first sc made, fasten off. Don't worry if the patt rep does not fit exactly!

BORDER

Round 1: Join A to any st along top of pillow, ch1, 1sc into same space, 1sc into every st evenly around pillow, working 3sc into every corner space. (approx. 48 sts along each side, don't worry if it is not exact)
Round 2: Ch3 (counts as 1dc), 1dc into next st, ch1, skip 1 st, *1dc into each of next 2 sts, ch1, skip 1 st; rep from *around edge, join with a sl st to top of ch 3, fasten off A.
Round 3: Join B to any ch 1 space in rnd 2, ch1, (1sc, ch3, 2dc), in same space and in every ch 1 space around edge, join with a sl st to first sc, fasten off.

MINI GRANNY SQUARES PILLOW

Make 25 squares in total; 9 with B centers, 8 with C centers, and 8 with D centers.
Using a center color, ch6, join with a sl st to form a ring.
Round 1: Ch3 (counts as 1dc), 2dc into ring, ch1, *3dc into ring, ch1; rep from * twice more, join rnd with a sl st to top of ch 3, fasten off, and weave in ends.
Round 2: Join A to any ch 1 space, ch3 (counts as 1dc), (2dc, ch2, 3dc) into same space as ch 3, ch1, *(3dc, ch1, 3dc), into next space, ch1; rep from * twice more, join rnd with a sl st to top of ch 3, fasten off, and weave in ends.

TO MAKE UP
Weave in ends (see page 125).

If you are a skilled sewist then you can make up your own fabric pillow covers, but it's easy to simply sew the crochet panels to ready-made pillow covers. I found it simplest to do this by hand with the covers still on the pads. I pinned the crochet panel in place, making sure the decorative border extended beyond the edges of the pillows, then from the back and using matching sewing thread, I slip-stitched the panel to the cover along the cover seam lines.

COLORFUL TWINE *Doormat*

This wonderful project is very much inspired by one of our loyal customers, Tina, who had created something similar for her camping trips. One thing that is immensely useful in a tent full of kids is a doormat to encourage everyone to realise that this might be a good place to take off their shoes! Being keen campers ourselves, it seemed sensible to give it a go, and it fits in perfectly at home, as well. There are many types and colors of twine, which is perfect for sturdy, hardwearing crochet—although I'm not sure I'd want to wear it! This is a super-simple design, just granny stripes with a border, but looks really lovely, and you can easily knock up another if it gets too dirty!

Yarn

Nutscene Heritage Jute Twine, 120yd (110m) spools

2 spools in Natural (A)

1 spool in Pink (B)

1 spool in Saffron (C)

1 spool in Lilac (D)

1 spool in Dove (E)

Note that 4 or 5 spools in total would be enough if using fewer colors

Hook and equipment

US I/9 (5.5mm) crochet hook

Large tapestry needle

Size

32 x 20¾in (81 x 53cm)

Gauge

3 groups of 3 doubles and 4.5 rows over 4in (10cm) using US I/9 (5.5mm) crochet hook

Abbreviations

See page 114

DOORMAT

Using A, ch92 (stitch patt is a multiple of 4).

Row 1: 2dc into 4th ch from hook, ch1, skip 3 ch, *3dc into next ch, ch1, skip 3 ch; rep from * to end of row, working 3dc into last ch, fasten off, turn. *(23 groups of 3dc)*

Row 2: Join in B, ch4 (counts as 1 dc, ch1), 3dc into first ch 1 space, * ch1, 3dc into next ch 1 space; rep from * to end of row, finishing with 1 group of 3dc into last ch 1 space, ch1, 1dc into top of ch 3, fasten off, turn. *(22 groups of 3dc)*

Row 3: Join in A, ch3 (counts as 1 dc), 2dc into the first ch 1 space, * ch1, 3dc into next ch 1 space; rep from * to end of row, finishing with 3dc into last ch 4 space, fasten off, turn. *(23 groups of 3dc)*

Rep rows 2–3 until 25 rows have been worked in total, or as many rows as required, alternating colors in the foll sequence: A, B, A, C, A, D, A, E, beginning with a C row and finishing with an A row, do not fasten off.

BORDER

Round 1: Ch1, 1sc into same place, 1sc into next st and into every st around the mat, working 3sc into each corner, join rnd with a sl st into first sc made, fasten off.

Round 2: Join in C, ch1, 1sc into same place, 1sc into each of next 2 sts, *ch3, sl st into 3rd ch, skip 1 st, 1sc into each of next 3 sts; rep from * to end of rnd, fasten off.

TO MAKE UP

Weave in ends (see page 125).

HOT WATER BOTTLE *Cover*

When you are feeling low, or cold, or maybe a bit of both, what could be better than cuddling up with a hot water bottle enclosed in a super-soft, super-gorgeous, hand-crocheted cover? I'm feeling better already! This is a lovely use of three muted colors, but you can have as much fun as you want with your own choices. The tiny squares have been crocheted together, which gives a really neat finish and also gives a lovely ridge around each square. You can have the ridge on the inside if you prefer, it makes no difference to the finished product.

Yarn

Mrs Moon Plump DK (80% superfine merino wool, 20% baby alpaca) light-worsted-weight (double knitting) yarn, 1¾oz (50g), 125yd (115m) skeins

2 skeins in Pavlova (A)
1 skein in Earl Grey (B)
1 skein in Gooseberry Fool (C)

Hook and equipment

US G/6 or H/8 (4.5mm) crochet hook
Large tapestry needle

Size

8¼in (21cm) wide and 11in (28cm) high (unstretched) to fit a standard hot water bottle

Gauge

Each granny square measures 2¾in (7cm) square

Abbreviations

See page 114

SQUARE

SQUARE A
Make 13 squares as folls: Round 1: B. Round 2: C. Round 3: A.

SQUARE B
Make 16 squares as folls: Round 1: C. Round 2: B. Round 3: A.

Using first color, ch6, join with a sl st to form a ring.
Round 1: Ch3 (counts as 1 dc), 2dc into ring, *ch2, 3dc into ring; rep from * twice more, finishing with ch2, join with a sl st to top of first ch 3, fasten off.
Round 2: Join second color to any ch 2 space, ch3 (counts as 1 dc), (2dc, ch2, 3dc) into same ch 2 space, ch1, *(3dc, ch2, 3dc) into foll ch 2 space, ch1; rep from * twice more, after final ch1 join rnd with a sl st to top of ch 3, fasten off.
Round 3: Join A to any ch 2 space, ch3 (counts as 1 dc), (2dc, ch2, 3dc) into same ch 2 space, *ch1, 3dc into next ch 1 space, ch1, (3dc, ch2, 3dc) into next ch 2 space; rep twice more from * to final corner, 3dc into final ch 1 space, ch1, join with a sl st to top of ch 3, fasten off A.

TO MAKE UP
Weave in ends (see page 125).
You can sew the squares together, though I have crocheted them together by slip stitching. I find this method quicker and easier, as I am rubbish at sewing; and it is easy to pull back if you go wrong.
To make the front, arrange 15 C-center squares in five rows of three squares (see diagram, right). With wrong sides together (so that the slip stitch ridge is on the right side), join all the horizontal rows to form long strips, slip stitching into the back

loop only of each square. Then join the long strips to form the rectangle. Attach the remaining C-center square to top of the central square, as shown.

To make the back, arrange 12 B-center squares in four rows of three squares. Join them as for the front and then attach the remaining square to the top.

Place both sides wrong sides together, carefully matching up the stitches. Starting at the LH side of the top, join the pieces by working 1sc into each stitch, going through both loops of the stitch on each piece. Work sc2tog into the inner corner and 4sc into the outer corner down the LH side. Leave the bottom flap open. Rejoin yarn on RH side and work as for the LH side.

You can leave the flap as it is and tuck it in once the hot water bottle is inside, but if you prefer you can sew two buttons on the outside of the shorter back side of the cover. Position the buttons so that you can fasten them into existing spaces in the granny squares.

Front

Back

FLOWER *Blanket*

The sublime colors of the Sweet Georgia yarn in this blanket give it a fabulously retro, yet timeless feel. It is the kind of throw that you can imagine being on a sofa for years, cuddling generations and remaining a constant in changing lives. The clever stitch pattern creates flowers that interlock. The petals of each flower are easily created by doubling two stitches together so although the pattern looks rather complicated, it is in fact very easy to get the hang of, and the chart shows you how the flowers link together.

You can of course make this blanket as large as you like: if you want to practice first, why not make a small pillow cover or even a scarf? As always, have fun with colors—find a yarn that you love and go wild!

Yarn

Sweet Georgia Superwash DK (100% superwash merino wool) light-worsted-weight (double-knitting) yarn, 4oz (115g), 256yd (234m) skeins

3 skeins in Birch (A)

1(2) skein(s) in Saffron (B) (see border note in patt)

1 skein in Bison (C)

1 skein in Dutch (D)

Hook and equipment

US F/5 or G/6 (4mm) crochet hook

Large tapestry needle

Size

Approx. 34 x 39in (86 x 100cm)

Gauge

2 flowers plus 2 sts and 7 rows over 4in (10cm) using US F/5 or G/6 (4mm) crochet hook

Abbreviations

See page 114

BLANKET

Using A, ch 201 loosely. (Stitch patt is a multiple of 11 + 3.)

Row 1 (RS): 1sc into 2nd ch from hook, ch1, skip 1 ch, 1sc into next ch, [ch3, skip 3 ch, 1sc into next ch] twice, *ch2, skip 2 ch, 1sc into next ch, [ch3, skip 3 ch, 1sc into next ch] twice; rep from * to last 2 ch, ch1, skip 1 ch, work 1sc into last ch, turn.

Row 2: Ch3, (dc2tog, ch2, dc2tog) into first ch 1 space, ch1, skip 1sc and ch 3 space, 1sc into next sc, *ch1, skip ch 3 space, [dc2tog, ch2] 3 times into next ch 2 space then dc2tog (still into same ch 2 space), ch1, skip 1sc and ch 3 space, 1sc into next sc; rep from * to last 2 sets of spaces, ch1, skip ch 3 space, (dc2tog, ch2, dc2tog) in ch 1 space, dc into last sc, fasten off A, turn.

Row 3: Join in B, ch1, 1sc into first sc, *ch3, 1dc2tog into top of each of next 4 dc2tog, ch3, 1sc into ch 2 space (this should be ch 2 space in middle space of 4 dc2tog from row 2); rep from * to end, working last sc into top of ch 3.

Row 4: Ch1, 1sc into first sc, *ch3, 1sc into top of first dc2tog, ch2, skip 2 dc2tog, 1sc into top of next dc2tog, ch3, 1sc into next sc; rep from * to end, finishing with 1sc into last sc, turn.

Row 5: Ch1, 1sc into first sc, *ch1, skip ch 3 space, [dc2tog, ch2] 3 times into next ch 2 space, then dc2tog (still into same ch 2 space), ch1, skip ch 3 space, 1sc into next sc; rep from * to end of row, finishing with 1sc into last sc, fasten off B, turn.

Row 6: Join in A, ch3, dc2tog into each of next 2 dc2tog, ch3, 1sc into next ch 2 space (that is the space between the 2nd and 3rd dc2tog of row 5), ch3, *dc2tog into next 4 dc2tog, ch3, 1sc into next ch 2 space, ch3; rep * to end of row, finishing with dc2tog into each of last 2 dc2tog, 1dc into last sc, turn.

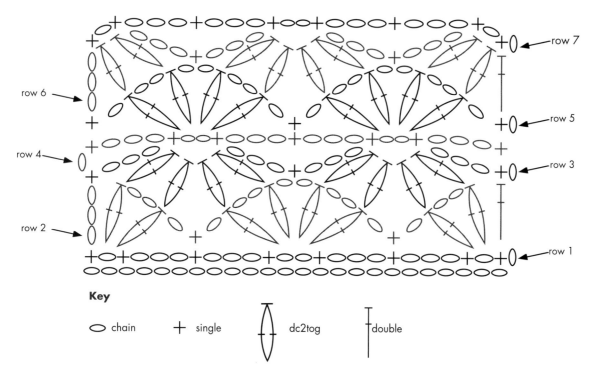

row 7
row 6
row 5
row 4
row 3
row 2
row 1

Key

⬭ chain   + single   ⬯ dc2tog   ⊤ double

Row 7: Ch1, 1sc into first dc, ch1, skip 1 dc2tog, 1sc into next dc2tog, ch3, 1sc into next sc, ch3, *1sc into next dc2tog, ch2, skip 2 dc2tog, 1sc into next dc2tog, ch3, 1sc into next sc, ch3; rep from * to last 2 dc2tog, work 1 sc into first of these, ch1, 1sc into top of ch3, turn.

Rep rows 2–7, changing to C on row 9, then back to A for foll 3 rows, then to D for next 3 rows. Cont in stitch patt as set, alternating the colors B, C, D every 3 rows with 3 rows of A in between each of those colors until 6 D stripes have been worked. Work 1 more row in A.

BORDER

The border is worked in B, though only a little of a second skein is needed for the pattern as written, so you could make a much more substantial border if you wish. If you prefer no border, then a second skein of B is not needed.

Round 1: Join yarn to top RH corner, ch1, 1sc into same space, work 1 rnd of sc evenly around edge of blanket, working 3sc into same stitch in every corner. Finish rnd by joining with a sl st to top of first sc.

Round 2 (picot round): *Ch3, sc into 3rd ch from hook (1 picot made), skip next st, sl st into foll st to secure picot to edge, sl st into next 2 sts; rep from * around blanket, fasten off.

TO MAKE UP

Weave in ends (see page 125).

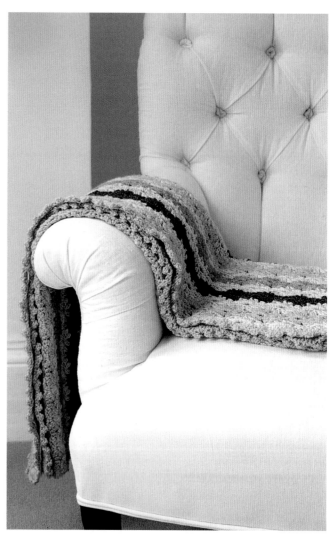

TEXTURED *Pillow*

Crochet is great for creating texture. All sorts of bumps and bobbles can be made really easily, and they produce beautiful effects on the simplest of items. This giant pillow is a case in point. The simple bobbles are made by crocheting four doubles together. It's very easy once you've done it once, and the bobbles are really effective. I've used two muted tones in stripes that accentuate the differences in texture, but keep the pillow looking stylish. You could go for a brighter, more contrasting stripe for a jazzier pillow, according to taste!

Yarn

West Yorkshire Spinners Re:Treat (100% wool) bulky-weight (chunky) yarn, 3½oz (100g), 153yd (140m) balls

3 balls in Harmony 184 (A)
4 balls in Joy 151 (B)

Other materials

23½in (60cm) square pillow pad

Hook and equipment

US K/10½ (7mm) crochet hook
Large tapestry needle

Size

23½in (60cm) square

Gauge

9 sts and 7 rows over houndstooth patt over 10cm (4in) using US K/10½ (7mm) crochet hook

Abbreviations

MB = make bobble by working dc4tog into same space.
See also page 114

PILLOW FRONT

Using A, ch51. (Stitch patt is a multiple of 4 + 3.)

Row 1(RS): 1dc into 4th ch from hook, 1dc into next ch and into every ch to end of row, fasten off, turn.

Row 2: Join in B, ch1 (does not count as st), 1sc into each of the first 2 sts, *MB in next st, 1sc into each of next 3 sts; rep from * to last 3 sts, MB in next st, 1 sc into next st, 1sc into top of ch 3, fasten off, turn.

Row 3: Join in A, ch3 (counts as 1 dc), skip st at base of ch 3, 1dc into next st, *1sc into top of bobble, 1dc into each of next 3 sts; rep from * to end of row, finishing with 1sc in top of last bobble, 1dc into each of last 2 sts, fasten off, turn.

Row 4: Join in B, ch1, 1sc into same place, 1sc into each of next 3 sts, *MB in next st , 1sc into each of next 3 sts; rep from * to end of row, 1sc in top of ch 3, fasten off, turn.

Row 5: Join in A, ch3 (counts as 1 dc), skip st at base of ch 3, *1dc into each of next 3 sts, 1sc into top of bobble; rep from * to end of row, finishing with 1dc into each of last 4 sts.

Rep rows 2–5 until work measures 23½in (60cm) or the size of the pillow pad, finishing with either a row 3 or 5. I am a loose crocheter and have worked 20 bobble rows but you should have plenty of yarn if you need to do more rows.

Next row (fold row): Join in B, ch1, 1 sc into same place, 1sc into next st and into every st to end of row, turn.

You should be working sc onto the dc from the row below and dc onto the sc from the row below; this alternating of stitches gives the houndstooth effect.

If you are doing a different-size pillow and the base number of stitches is even, then every row starts with a dc (that is, ch3) and finishes with a sc.

TO MAKE UP

Weave in ends (see page 125).

Right side in, fold the pillow in half along the fold row. Work a row of sl st along the edge just worked and then evenly down one side (as a general rule work one stitch in the side of a sc and two into the side of a dc). Turn the pillow right side out, insert the pillow pad and then, using A, sew up the final edge.

PILLOW BACK

Next row: Join in A, ch3 (counts as 1 dc), skip st at base of ch 3, *1sc into next st, 1dc into next st, rep from * to end of row, finishing with 1dc into last st, fasten off, turn.

Next row: Join in B, ch1, 1sc into same place, *1dc into next st, 1sc into foll st; rep from * to end of row, finishing with 1sc into last st, turn.

Rep last 2 rows until back matches front in length, finishing with an A row, do not fasten off.

Making up the pillow

I've given a contrast pattern for the back of the pillow, but you could easily back it with fabric if you prefer.

SUPER *Rug*

Super-simple, super-fabulous, and super-quick! This is a great, giant project that you can finish in a couple of hours. The very thick yarn grows incredibly quickly and is great fun to work with. Despite its size, this is just a very simple pattern, which could equally be a placemat if you used a fingering yarn! After creating a basic circle of doubles, the fun border is added in a contrast color to give the whole thing real zing. Enjoy!

Yarn

Rowan Big Wool (100% merino wool) super-bulky-weight (super chunky) yarn, 3½oz (100g), 87yd (80m) balls

  2 balls in Ice Blue 21 (A)

  3 balls in Pantomime 79 (B)

Hook and equipment

US S/35 (20mm) crochet hook

Large tapestry needle

Size

35¾in (90cm) diameter

Gauge

4.5 dc sts and 2 dc rows over 4in (10cm) using US S/35 (20mm) crochet hook

Abbreviations

MP = make picot. A picot is made by ch3 and then slip stitching into the 3rd ch from hook.

See page 114

CENTER OF RUG

Using A, ch8, join with a sl st to form a ring, being careful not to twist the chain.

Round 1: Ch3 (counts as 1 dc), work 14 dc into ring, join rnd with a sl st to top of ch 3. *(15 dc)*

Round 2: Ch3 (counts as 1 dc), 1dc into same place, 2dc into next st and into every st to end of rnd, join rnd with a sl st to top of ch 3. *(30 dc)*

Round 3: Ch3 (counts as 1 dc), 1dc into same place, 1dc into next st, *2dc into next st, 1 dc into next st; rep from * to end of rnd, join rnd with a sl st to top of ch 3. *(45 dc)*

Round 4: Ch3 (counts as 1 dc), 1dc into same place, 1dc into each of next 2 sts, *2dc into foll st, 1dc into each of next 2 sts; rep from * to end of rnd, join with a sl st to top of ch 3. *(60 dc)*

Round 5: Ch3 (counts as 1 dc), 1dc into same place, 1dc into each of next 3 sts, *2dc into foll st, 1dc into each of next 3 sts; rep from * to end of rnd, join with a sl st to top of ch 3. *(75 sts)*

Round 6: Ch3 (counts as 1 dc), 1dc into same place, 1dc into each of next 4 sts, *2dc into foll st, 1dc into each of next 4 sts; rep from * to end of rnd, join with a sl st to top of ch 3. *(90 dc)*

Fasten off A.

PINK EDGING

Round 1: Join in B, ch1 (does not count as st), 1sc into same place, *ch3, skip 2 sts, 1sc into next st, ch1, skip 1 st, 1sc into next st; rep from * to end of rnd, finishing with ch1, skip last st, join with a sl st to the first sc made.

Round 2: Sl st twice into first ch 3 space (to get to the right place to start this rnd), ch3 (counts as 1 dc), 3dc into ch 3 space, *1dc into next ch 1 space, 4dc into next ch 3 space; rep from * to end of rnd, finish with 1dc into last ch 1 space, join with sl st to top of ch 3.

Round 3: Sl st in next st (to get to the right place to start this rnd), ch1 (does not count as st), 1sc into same st, *ch1, skip next dc, 1sc into foll dc, ch3, skip 2 dc, 1sc into next dc; rep from * finishing with ch 3, join with a sl st to first sc made.

Round 4: Sl st into next ch 1 space, ch6, sl st into 3rd ch from hook (1dc and picot made), * (1dc, ch1, 1dc (MP), ch1, 1dc (MP), ch1, 1dc) in foll ch 3 space, (1dc (MP)) into foll ch 1 space; rep from * to end of rnd, finishing after a ch 3 space, join with sl st to 3rd ch of ch 6.

TO MAKE UP

Weave in ends (see page 125); you will probably need to do this with your fingers!

CAMPING *Throw*

This is the ultimate easy-to-make crochet project—a fabulous, brightly colored, enormous granny square, finished with a great fun border. It is a perfect blanket and you will have it for years and years, be it as a picnic blanket, a baby blanket, a throw for the sofa, a bedspread, or an essential camping companion, which is what I use this one as! I've used a hard-wearing yarn that you don't need to worry about being used and abused—it can take it!

Yarn

Cascade 220 Superwash (100% wool) worsted-weight (Aran) yarn, 3½oz (100g), 219yd (200m) balls

2 balls in Daisy Yellow 346 (A)
2 balls in Blaze 9552 (B)
2 balls in Peach 1940 (C)
1 ball in Really Red 809 (D1)
1 ball in Christmas Red Heather 1922 (D2)
2 balls in Pink Ice 836 (E)
1 ball in White 871 (F1)
1 ball in Aran 817 (F2)

Hook and equipment

US G/6 or H/8 (4.5mm) crochet hook
Large tapestry needle

Size

48½ x 48½in (123 x 123cm)

Gauge

5 groups of 3dc and 4 ch2 spaces, and 8 rows over 4in (10cm) using US G/6 or H/8 (4.5mm) crochet hook

Abbreviations

See page 114

BLANKET

Using A, ch6, join with a sl st to form a ring.
Round 1: Ch3 (counts as 1 dc), 2dc into ring, *ch2, 3dc into ring; rep from * twice more finishing with a ch2, join with a sl st to top of first ch 3, fasten off.
Round 2: Join B to any ch 2 space, ch3 (counts as 1 dc), (2dc, ch2, 3dc) into same ch 2 space, ch1, *(3dc, ch2, 3dc) into foll ch 2 space work, ch1; rep from * twice more, after final ch1 join rnd with a sl st to top of ch 3, fasten off.
Round 3: Join C to any ch 2 space, ch3 (counts as 1 dc), (2dc, ch2, 3dc) into same ch 2 space, *ch1, 3dc into next ch 1 space, ch1, (3dc, ch2, 3dc) into next ch 2 space; rep from * twice more to final corner, work 3dc into final ch 1 space, ch1, join with a sl st to top of ch 3, fasten off.
Round 4: Join D1 to any ch 2 space, ch3 (counts as 1 dc), (2dc, ch2, 3dc) into same ch 2 space, *(ch1, 3dc) into next two ch 1 spaces, ch1, (3dc, ch2, 3dc) into next ch 2 space; rep from *

Choosing yarns

Granny square blankets are traditionally made up of leftover scraps of yarn—hence their garishness—and I have given a nod to that tradition here. I bought a few colors first and when I went back to buy more, I could no longer get hold of a couple of shades, so you will see that there are two reds and a cream and a white. I wanted to show that precise colors really don't matter; the blanket looks absolutely amazing and a little bit of imperfection makes it all the more perfect!

twice more, after final corner space, (ch1, 3dc) into each of final two ch 1 spaces, ch1, join the round with a sl st to top of ch 3.
Round 5 and beyond: Rep row 4 using E. As the blanket grows, there will be more ch 1 side spaces and cont working 3dc into each of these, separated by a ch1. In each of the four corner spaces work (3dc, ch2, 3dc). Change color every round in the sequence A, B, C, D, E, switching from D1 to D2 when necessary.

BORDER

Round 1: Join F1 to any ch 2 corner space, work one ordinary granny square row, as above, do not fasten off, do not turn.
Round 2: Ch1, 1sc into same place, 1sc into each of next 2 sts, into ch 2 space work (2sc, ch2, 2sc), cont working a sc round by working 1sc into each dc, 1sc into each ch 1 space and into each ch 2 corner space work (2sc, ch2, 2sc), finishing rnd by joining with a sl st to top of first sc, do not turn.
Round 3: Ch1, 1sc into same place, 1sc into each of next 4 sts, into ch 2 corner space work (2sc, ch2, 2sc), cont around, working 1sc into every st and (2sc, ch2, 2sc) into each corner space, join rnd with a sl st to top of first sc, fasten off yarn, do not turn.

Round 4 (picot fan): Join F2 to any ch 2 corner space, ch6 (counts as 1 dc, ch 3), [1dc, ch3] 3 more times into same ch 2 corner space, 1dc into same ch 2 corner space to finish fan, skip 2 sts, 1sc into foll st, *skip 3 sts, (1dc, ch3) into foll st 5 times, finish with 1dc into same st, skip 3 sts, 1sc into foll st; rep from * around blanket.

You should be working the last fan before every corner in about the 6th st before the ch 2 corner space: work the fan in this st, skip 3 sts, 1sc into next st, skip 1 st then work the corner fan, after the corner fan skip 1 st, 1sc into foll st and then rep from * to next corner. However, do not worry if this is not exactly the case! If the fan is worked in the 8th st before the corner, just make sure you skip 3 sts and make 1 sc into next st. If after this you have more or fewer than 1 st before the corner space, it will not show in the finished blanket. Finish rnd with last sc before corner, sl st into 3rd ch of ch 6, fasten off yarn.

TO MAKE UP
Weave in ends (see page 125).
Press the blanket.

No color change
If you do not want to change color every round, you need to sl st into each of next 3dc and into the ch 2 space, then work as instructed. You must move to next space along as every round starts in a space.

CHAPTER 4

Accessories

The small size of accessory projects means that they are pleasingly quick to make, even if you are using finer yarn than for blankets or sweaters. And you can easily crochet with materials other than conventional yarn; the very practical—yet still good-looking—shopping bag in this chapter is made from jute twine!

PUFF *Mitts*

There are times when crochet needs to look a little less like crochet—needs to lose that laciness and make a fabric that is a bit more knit-like. Mittens are a case in point; to fulfil their basic role as handwarmers, they need a bit more structure than crochet normally gives. I hope that these mittens have solved that problem. They are a bit more tricky than a lot of the projects in this book, but once you are familiar with the stitch pattern it isn't actually difficult, so practice with some spare yarn before starting the project. I'd really recommend giving the mitts a go; they are so lovely when finished!

Yarn

Mrs Moon Plump DK (80% superfine merino wool, 20% baby alpaca) light worsted-weight (double knitting) yarn, 1¾oz (50g), 125yd (115m) skeins
    1 skein in Gooseberry Fool

Hook and equipment

US F/5 or G/6 (4mm) crochet hook
Large tapestry needle

Size

8in (20cm) long (including trim) and 3½in (9cm) wide (unstretched)

Gauge

15 sc sts and 12 sc rows over 4in (10cm) using US F/5 or G/6 (4mm) crochet hook
15 hdc sts and 12 hdc rnds over 4in (10cm) using US F/5 or G/6 (4mm) crochet hook

Abbreviations

See page 114

LEFT-HAND MITTEN

CUFF

Ch11 loosely.
Row 1: Work 1sc into 2nd ch from hook, 1sc in every ch to end, turn. *(10 sts)*
Row 2: Ch1 (does not count as st), 1sc in BLO of same space, work 1sc BLO into next st and into each st to end of row, turn. *(10 sts)*
Rep row 2 until 28 rows in total have been worked, do not fasten off.
Place the two ends together and join seam by working a sl st through each st across first and last rows to form a tube, do not fasten off. This is the cuff finished!
Turn the cuff counter-clockwise 90 degrees.

HAND

Round 1: Ch1, 1sc into same space, work 1sc into end of each row around cuff (28 sts in total), join rnd with a sl st into top of first sc made, do not turn, cont working in the round throughout.
Round 2: Ch2 (counts as 1 hdc), work 1hdc into next st and into every st to end of rnd, join rnd with a sl st to top of ch 2, do not turn. *(28 sts)*
Rep rnd 2 until 8 complete hdc rnds have been worked. Try the mitt on now to see if it is long enough to start the thumbhole; if not work as many more rnds of hdc as needed.**

MAKE THUMBHOLE

Round 9: Ch2 (counts as 1 hdc), 1hdc into next st, ch6, skip 5 sts, work 1hdc into next st and into every st to end of rnd, join with a sl st to top of ch 2.
Round 10: Ch2 (counts as 1 hdc), 1hdc into next st, work 5hdc into ch 6 space, 1hdc into next st and into every st to end of rnd, join with a sl st to top of ch 2. *(28 sts)*
***Work three straight hdc rnds (as for rnd 2). Try mitt on to see it it fits, and work more rnds if needed.
Round 14: Ch1 (does not count as st), 1sc into same space, work 1sc into next st and into each st to end of rnd, join rnd with a sl st to top of first sc. *(28sts)*

Mitten structure

You begin by making a crochet rib, which is a great technique to have mastered. The rib is worked sideways and then joined into a tube before starting the main body of the mitt. The mitts are both worked the same way other than the position of the thumb, which is placed on each mitt so that the "seam" that appears as you move up rows is on the palm rather than the top of each mitt. Working into the back loop only (BLO) of each stitch creates a lovely, stretchy fabric. The shell trim and thumbs are optional. Consider using a contrast color for the rib and shell edging, or make the rib extra-long for a more luxurious pair of mittens. Remember to purchase extra yarn if you plan on lengthening the mittens.

Round 15 (shell trim): Ch1 (does not count as st), sl st into same space, *skip one st, work 5 hdc into next st, skip one st, sl st into next st; rep from * to end of rnd, working final sl st into first sl st made to join, fasten off, and weave in ends. *(7 shells)*

MAKE THUMB

Join yarn to first hdc (on RH side of hole), ch2 (counts as 1 hdc) work 1hdc into each of the 4 sts, then work 7 hdc evenly around the other side of the thumbhole, join with a sl st to top of ch2. *(12 sts)*
If this looks like too many or too few stitches, just add or subtract sts evenly until there are as many as looks right.
Thumb row 2: Ch2 (counts as 1 hdc), work 1hdc into each st around, join with a sl st to top of ch 2.
Thumb row 3: Ch1, 1sc into same space, 1 sc into every st around, join with a sl st to first sc made, fasten off.

RIGHT-HAND MITTEN

Work as for left-hand mitten to **.

MAKE THUMBHOLE

Round 9: Ch2 (counts as 1 hdc), 1hdc into each of next 20 sts, ch6, skip 5 sts, 1hdc in each of last 2 sts, join with a sl st to top of ch 2.
Round 10: Ch2 (counts as 1 hdc), 1hdc into each st to ch 6 space, work 5hdc into ch 6 space, 1hdc in each of last 2 sts, join with a sl st to top of ch 2. *(28 sts)*
Work as for left-hand mitten from *** to end.

TO MAKE UP

Weave in ends (see page 125).

PUFF BOBBLE *Beret*

This fun beret has a distinctly Celtic feel to it, but without the pompom and mix of colors it has a more Parisian vibe... it's up to you to decide which you prefer. This is a lovely small project and great if you've never done puffs before. They have real depth and give a completely different look to crochet, creating a fabric that looks as though it's been woven rather than crocheted. The beret is worked in the round, so there is no seaming to do afterward. This also gives a beautiful look on the top of the beret where all the increases radiate out from the middle.

Yarn

Berroco Ultra Alpaca (50% alpaca, 50% wool), worsted-weight (Aran) yarn, 3½oz (100g), 217yd (198m) balls
1 ball in Grapefruit Mix 62178 (A)
1 ball in Tea Rose 62114 (B)

Hooks and equipment

US G/6 or H/8 (4.5mm) and US H/8 or I/9 (5mm) crochet hooks
Large tapestry needle

Size

One size: 8in (20cm) high (not including pompom), and 19¾in (48cm) circumference at rim (unstretched)

Gauge

7 puffs and 8 rows over 4in (10cm) using US H/8 or I/9 (5mm) crochet hook

Abbreviations

PUFF = hdc4tog in same space, yoh and pull through to secure.
See also page 114

BERET

Using A, make a crochet magic ring.
Round 1: Using US H/8 or I/9 (5mm) hook, ch1, work 6sc into the ring, pull ring tight, and join round with a sl st into top of 1st sc made.
Round 2: Ch2 (counts as 1 hdc), hdc3tog (this with the ch2 counts as first PUFF) into 1st sc, *ch1, PUFF into next sc; rep from * to end, after last PUFF do not ch1, but 1dc into top of first PUFF made to finish round (1dc acts as the last space between puffs and no sl st is required to join the round; working the dc here gets you neatly in the right place to start next rnd).
Round 3: Ch2 (counts as 1 hdc), hdc3tog in same space working around the dc of the previous row (this is the space between 6th and 1st PUFF of rnd 2), ch1, 1 PUFF into same space, *ch1, (1 PUFF, ch1, 1 PUFF) into next ch1 space (between PUFFs of previous rnd); rep from * to end of rnd, join with 1dc to top of 1st PUFF.

Round 4: Ch2 (counts as 1 hdc), hdc3tog around dc, ch1, (PUFF, ch1, PUFF) into next ch 1 space, *ch1, 1 PUFF into next ch 1 space, ch1, (PUFF, ch1, PUFF) into next ch 1 space; rep from * to end of rnd, join with 1dc to top of 1st PUFF.

Round 5: Ch2 (counts as 1 hdc), hdc3tog around dc, ch1, 1 PUFF into next ch 1 space, ch1, (PUFF, ch1, PUFF) into next ch 1 space, (this should be in the ch 1 in (PUFF, ch1, PUFF) from the previous rnd), *ch1, (1 PUFF, ch1) into each of next two ch 1 spaces, (PUFF, ch1, PUFF) into next ch 1 space; rep from * to end of rnd, join with 1dc to top of 1st PUFF.

Round 6: Ch2 (counts as 1 hdc), hdc3tog around dc, ch1, (1 PUFF, ch1) into each of next two ch 1 spaces, (PUFF, ch1, PUFF) into next space, *ch1, (1 PUFF, ch1) into each of next three ch 1 spaces, (PUFF, ch1, PUFF) into next space; rep from * to end of rnd, join with 1dc to top of 1st PUFF.

Round 7: Ch2 (counts as 1 hdc), hdc3tog around dc, ch1, (1 PUFF, ch1) into each of next three ch 1 spaces, (PUFF, ch1, PUFF) into next ch 1 space, *ch1, (1 PUFF, ch1) into each of next four ch 1 spaces, (PUFF, ch1, PUFF) into next space; rep from * to end of rnd, join with 1dc to top of 1st PUFF.

Round 8: Ch2 (counts as 1 hdc), hdc3tog around dc, ch1 (1 PUFF, ch1) into each of next four ch 1 spaces, (PUFF, ch1, PUFF) into next ch 1 space, *ch1, (PUFF, ch1) into each of next five ch 1 spaces, (PUFF, ch1, PUFF) into next ch 1 space; rep from * to end of rnd, join with 1dc to top of 1st PUFF.

Round 9: Ch2 (counts as 1 hdc), hdc3tog around dc, ch1, (PUFF, ch1) into each of next five spaces, (PUFF, ch1, PUFF) into next ch 1 space, *ch1, (PUFF, ch1) into each of next six spaces, (PUFF, ch1, PUFF) into next ch 1 space; rep from * to end of rnd, join with 1dc to top of 1st PUFF.

Round 10 (straight): Ch2 (counts as 1 hdc), hdc3tog around dc, (ch1, PUFF) into each ch 1 space to end of rnd, join with 1dc to top of 1st PUFF. *(48 PUFF)*

Rounds 11–12: Rep rnd 10.

Round 13 (smaller PUFF): Ch2, hdc2tog around dc, (ch1, hdc3tog) into each ch 1 space to end of rnd, join with 1dc to top of 1st PUFF, do not fasten off. *(48 PUFF)*

BAND

Round 1: Using US G/6 or H/8 (4.5mm) hook, ch1, 1sc around dc, 1sc into top of next PUFF, *1sc into next ch 1 space, 1sc into top of next PUFF; rep from * to end, join with a sl st to top of 1st sc, fasten off A. *(96 sts)*

Round 2: Join in B, ch1, 1sc into same place and 1sc into every st to end of rnd, join with a sl st to top of 1st sc, fasten off B.

Round 3 (decrease rnd): Join in A, ch1, 1sc into same place, *1sc into each of next 3 sts, sc2tog; rep from * to end of rnd, join with a sl st to top of 1st sc, fasten off A.
(77 sts)

Rounds 4–8: Rep rnd 2, alternating color on every row.

If the hat is too tight, do not work as many rounds on the rim. If it is too loose, work another rnd 3.

TO MAKE UP
Weave in ends (see page 125).

POMPOM
Using both A and B together, make a pompom and attach it to the center of the beret by threading the ends of yarn used to tie the pompom together through either side of the center of the beret and tying them tightly in a double knot. This helps avoid pompom wobble, which is disconcerting for all involved!

TWINE *Shopping Bag*

Like the Colorful Twine Doormat (see page 58), this project makes perfect use of this wonderfully colored, hard-wearing fiber! There are so many different color combinations you could go for, but equally, a natural bag seems right, too. Ours is very patriotic in its glorious red, white, and blue, but you could go for all sorts of color combinations depending on your mood or nation! The bag has a solid base, so that unlike the string bags of the '70s you can actually put things in this one without fear of them dropping out straight away! I've gone for short handles, but you can easily lengthen these if you want an over-the-shoulder version.

Yarn

Nutscene Heritage Twine, 120yd (110m)

2 spools in Ivory (A)

1 spool in Cornflower (B)

Note that you only require a small amount of B for the edging around the top of the base, and you can use A instead if you prefer.

Bakers Twine, 109yd (100m)

1 spool in Red, White, and Blue "Union Jack" (C)

Hook and equipment

US G/6 or H/8 (4.5mm) crochet hook

Large tapestry needle

Size

13¾in (35cm) high and 11in (28cm) wide

Gauge

10 dc sts and 5 dc rows over 4in (10cm) using US G/6 or H/8 (4.5mm) crochet hook

Abbreviations

See page 114

BAG

Using A, ch6, join with a sl st to form a ring, being careful not to twist the chain.

Round 1: Ch3 (counts as 1 dc), work 13dc into ring, join rnd with a sl st into top of ch 3, do not turn. *(14 sts)*

Round 2: Ch3 (counts as 1 dc), 1dc into same place, 2dc into next st and into every st to end of rnd, join rnd with sl st to top of ch 3. *(28 dc)*

Round 3: Ch3 (counts as 1 dc), 1dc into same place, 1dc into next st, *2dc into next st, 1dc into next st; rep from * to end of rnd, finishing with 1dc into last st, join with a sl st to top of ch 3. *(42 dc)*

Round 4: Ch3 (counts as 1 dc), 1dc into same place, 1 dc into each of next 2 sts, *2dc into next st, 1 dc into each of next 2 sts; rep from * to end of rnd, finishing with 1dc into each of last 2 sts, join with a sl st to top of ch 3. *(56 dc)*

Round 5: Ch3 (counts as 1 dc), 1dc into same place, 1 dc into each of next 3 sts, *2dc into next st, 1 dc into each of next 3 sts; rep from * to end of rnd, finishing with 1dc into each of last 3 sts, join with a sl st to top of ch 3. *(70 dc)*

Round 6: Ch3 (counts as 1 dc), 1dc into same place, 1 dc into each of next 4 sts, *2dc into next st, 1 dc into each of next 4 sts; rep from * to end of rnd, finishing with 1dc into each of last 3 sts, join with a sl st to top of ch 3. *(84 dc)*

Round 7: Ch3 (counts as 1 dc), 1dc into next st and into every st to end of rnd, join with a sl st to top of ch 3. *(84 dc)*

Round 8: Ch1, 1sc into same place, 1 sc into next st and into every st to end of rnd, join with a sl st to top of first sc, fasten off A.

Round 9: Join in B, ch1, 1sc into same place, 1 sc into next st and into every st to end of rnd, join with a sl st to top of first sc, fasten off B. Note that if you prefer, you can work this rnd in A.

Round 10: Join in C, ch1, 1sc into same place, *ch 5, skip 2sc, 1sc into next st, rep from * to last 2sc, skip 2sc, sl st to top of first sc.

Round 11: To get to the right place to start next rnd, sl st twice into next ch 5 space, ch1, 1sc into same ch 5 loop, *ch5, 1sc into next ch 5 loop; rep from * to end of rnd, ch5, sl st to top of first sc.
Rep rnd 11 until the bag is required length; this bag measured 14in (35cm) high with the netting slightly stretched. Fasten off B.

Rim round 1: Join A into any ch 5 space, ch3 (counts as 1 dc), 1dc into same sp, *1dc into next sc, 2dc into next space; rep from * around rim, join with a sl st to top of ch 3.

Rim round 2: Ch1, 1sc into same place, 1sc into next st and into every stitch to end of rnd, join with a sl st to top of first sc made, fasten off.

HANDLES
(Make two)
Using A, ch 50 (or length required).
Row 1: 1hdc into 3rd ch from hook and into every ch to end of row, fasten off.

TO MAKE UP
Weave in ends (see page 125).
Sew handles in place using A.

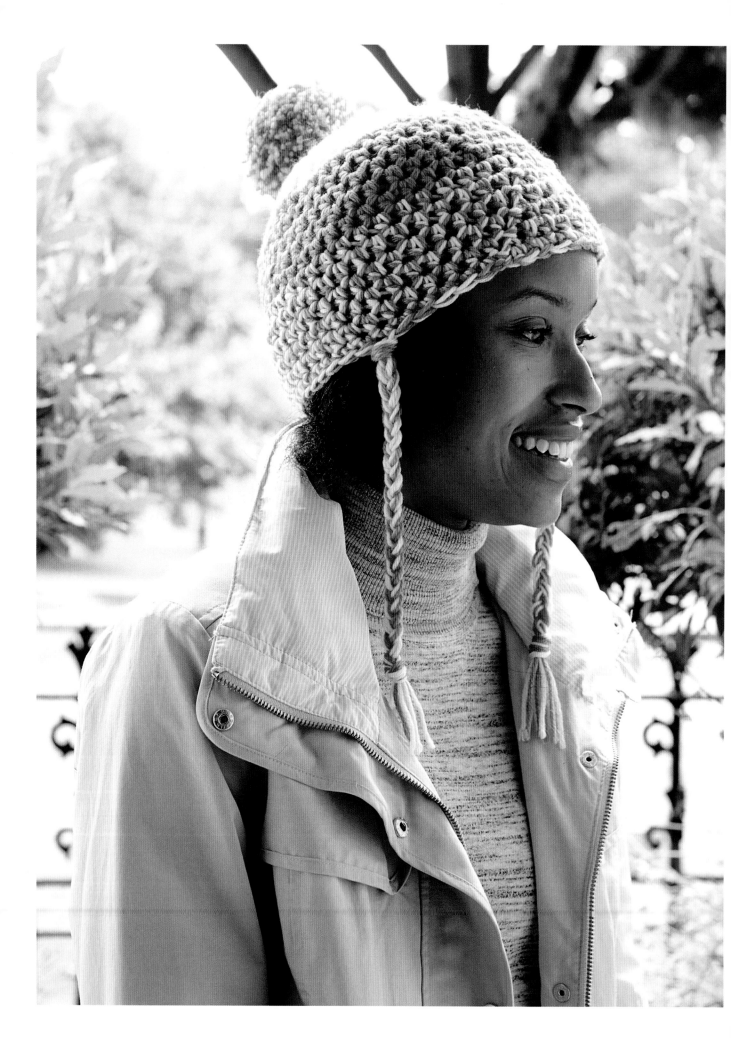

SNOWBOARDER'S *Hat*

You obviously don't need to snowboard to wear this hat, or even ski—to be honest it doesn't even need to be worn somewhere snowy... What I mean to imply by the name is that this hat is super-cool! I'm sure any snowboarder would love to wear it. It's also super-easy to make. The hat is crocheted in the round starting at the top, so there is no sewing up to be done at the end, and it's easy to make it bigger or smaller according to your needs.

Yarn

Debbie Bliss Rialto Aran (100% merino wool) worsted-weight (Aran) yarn, 1¾oz (50g), 85yd (78m) balls

3 balls in Ecru 2 (A)

3 balls in Ginger 6 (B)

Hook and equipment

US K/10½ (7mm) crochet hook

Large tapestry needle

Size

22in (56cm) circumference (to fit an average adult head) and 8¼in (21cm) from top to bottom

Gauge

9 hdc and 8 rows over 4in (10cm) using US K/10½ (7mm) crochet hook

Abbreviations

See page 114

HAT

Using 2 strands (take one from the center of the ball and one from the outside) of A, ch4, join with a sl st to form a ring.

Round 1: Ch2 (counts as 1 hdc), work 9 hdc into ring, join with a sl st to top of ch 2, do not turn. *(10 sts)*

Round 2: Ch2 (counts as 1 hdc), 1hdc into same st (at base of ch 2), 2hdc into next st (this is quite difficult to see as it looks very close to the ch 2), 2hdc into each st to end of rnd, join with a sl st to top of ch 2, do not turn. *(20 sts)*

Round 3: Ch2 (counts as 1 hdc), 1hdc into same st, 1hdc into next st, *2hdc into foll st, 1hdc into next st; rep from * to end of rnd, finishing with 1hdc in last st, join with a sl st to top of ch 2, do not turn. *(30 sts)*

Round 4: Ch2 (counts as 1 hdc), 1hdc into same st, *1hdc into each of next 2 sts, 2hdc into foll st; rep from * to end of rnd, finishing with 1hdc into each of last 2 sts, join with a sl st to top of ch 2, do not turn. *(40 sts)*

Round 5: Ch2 (counts as 1 hdc), 1hdc into same place *1hdc into each of next 3 sts, 2hdc into foll st; rep from * to end of rnd, finishing with 1hdc into each of last 3 sts, join with a sl st to top of ch 2, fasten off A, do not turn. *(50 sts)*

Break A and join in 2 strands of B, holding both strands together.

Round 6: Ch2 (counts as 1 hdc), 1hdc into foll st and into every st to end of rnd, join with a sl st to top of ch 2. *(50 sts)*

Rounds 7–15: Rep rnd 5. You can make the hat larger of smaller here, just keep trying it on for size. Work 5 rnds in total using B, then break 1 strand of B and join in 1 strand of A, holding A and B together. Work 5 rnds using A and B strands.

Round 16 (rim): Ch1, 1sc into same place, work 1sc into every st to end of rnd, join with a sl st to top of first sc made, fasten off yarn.

TO MAKE UP
Weave in ends (see page 125).

POMPOM
Make a pompom using both colors, keeping ends quite long after you have tied it and using these to attach the pompom to the hat.

PLAITS
(Make 2)
Cut 3 x 1m (1yd) lengths of both colors of yarn. Lay the 6 strands together, pick up in the middle, and using a crochet hook pull through the rim and hitch to make a long tassel. Plait the yarn (you should have 12 strands, so divide into groups of 4, mixing the colors); when it is the desired length, tie a knot, and trim ends. Repeat on opposite side of rim.

Choosing yarns
The hat is crocheted with two strands of yarn held together, using two different colors either on their own or mixed together. This gives such a great effect and adds a bit of fun to this lovely beanie.

PINWHEEL CLUTCH
Purse

This clutch purse is a great way to show off crochet at its best! The interlocking circles produced by pinwheel stitch create a really eye-catching geometric pattern, particularly when using a stark contrast in colors as I have done here. Pinwheels are very simple to create: you work groups of doubles together in one place—easy to achieve for a new crocheter. Any strong cotton yarn would work, and you can make the purse bigger by adding extra pattern reps from the start. There is a chart as well as the written pattern to help you work the stitch.

Yarn

Rico Essentials Cotton DK (100% cotton) light-worsted-weight (double knitting) yarn, 1¾oz (50g), 131yd (120m) balls
  1 ball in Cobalt Blue 32 (A)
  1 ball in White 80 (B)

Hooks and equipment

US C/2 (3mm) crochet hook and US G/6 or H/8 (4.5mm) crochet hook (for the handle)
Large tapestry needle

Size

5 x 10in (13 x 25cm)

Gauge

Each pinwheel measures 1¼ x 1¼in (3 x 3cm)

Abbreviations

See page 114

PURSE

Using US C/2 (3mm) crochet hook and A, ch56 loosely.

Row 1: 1sc into 2nd ch from hook, 1sc into next ch, *skip 3 ch, 7dc into foll ch, skip 3 ch, 1sc into each of next 3 ch; rep from * to end of row, finishing last 4 ch with skip 3 ch, 4dc into last ch, fasten off A, turn.

Row 2: Using B, ch1, 1sc into same place, 1sc into next st, *ch3, dc7tog, ch3, 1 sc into each of next 3 sts; rep from * to end of row, finishing with dc4tog over last 4 sts, turn.

Row 3: Ch3 (counts as 1 dc), 3dc into same place, *skip ch 3, 1sc into each of foll 3 sc, skip ch 3, 7dc into top of dc7tog; rep from * to end of row, finishing with skip ch 3, 1sc into each of last 2 sts, fasten off B, turn.

Row 4: Using A, ch3 (counts as 1 dc), skip st at the base of ch 3, dc3tog over next 3 sts, *ch3, 1sc into each of next 3 sts, ch3, dc7tog; rep from * to end of row, finishing with ch3, 1sc into last dc, and 1sc into top of ch 3, turn.

Row 5: Ch1, 1sc into same place, 1sc into next st, *skip ch 3, 7dc into top of dc7tog, skip ch 3, 1sc into each of next 3 sc; rep from * to end of row, finishing with 1sc into each of last 3 sc, skip ch 3, 4dc into top of 3dctog, fasten off A, turn.

Rep rows 2–5 until 17½ complete pinwheels (35 rows) have been worked, or it measures approx. 14in (35cm). Finish with a row 3 or 5 to make a scalloped edge for the fold-over flap.

TO MAKE UP

This purse has been made up so the wrong side is on the outside, as I preferred the pattern that way. However, whatever you decide, weave in the ends on the inside (see page 125). Fold up the lower third of the crochet, matching up the pattern along the edge. Sew the side seams. I measured out a piece of stiff card to fit inside the purse and covered this with fabric to give the purse some structure. Lining the purse with some contrasting fabric would also look great.

HANDLE LOOP

Using US G/6 or H/8 (4.5mm) crochet hook and two strands of B held together, join the yarn to the top RH corner of the purse (under the flap) ch35, join ch to purse in same place with a sl st, fasten off and weave in ends.

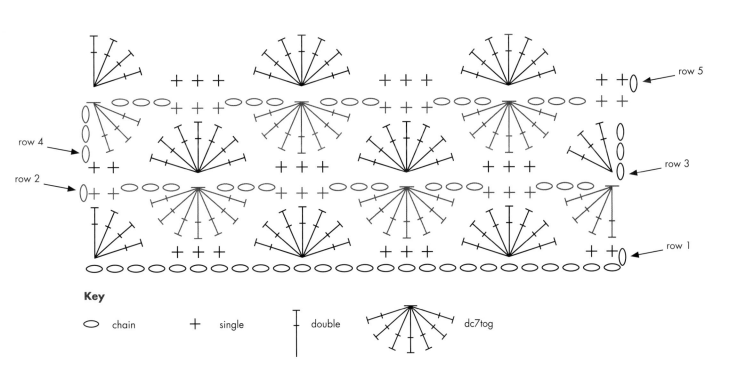

Key

⬭ chain   + single   ⊤ double   ⤬ dc7tog

MEDALLION *Choker*

Intricate crochet stitches really lend themselves to jewelry; they can be works of art in themselves and sometimes just need a bit of extra showing off. This beautiful choker mixes a crochet cotton with a silver thread that makes it looks as though it is actually made of metal, but has the benefit of being soft enough to wear. The choker is a simple four-row pattern, so this is a great project for gifts! You can get many out of one ball of each yarn. The roundels are created by working groups of doubles into loops; really not difficult at all and very effective! I'm making loads for my friends' birthdays this year. The crochet cotton has a gorgeous lustrous sheen, so if you prefer you can leave out the metallic thread.

Yarn

Rico Essentials Crochet Cotton (100% cotton) fingering (lace-weight) yarn, 1¾oz (50g), 284yd (260m) balls
  1 ball in Smoky Blue 17 (A)

Sajou Metallic Thread (100% polyester), 246yd (225m) spool
  1 spool in silver (B)

Hook and equipment

US B/1 (2.25mm) crochet hook
Large tapestry needle

Size

21in (53cm) long (including ties)

Gauge

Each roundel to measure approximately 1in (2.5cm) using US B/1 (2.25mm) crochet hook and one strand each of A and B held together

Abbreviations

See page 114

CHOKER

Use one strand each of A and B held together throughout. Ch112 loosely.

Row 1: 1sc into 2nd ch from hook, 1sc into every st to end of ch, turn.

Row 2: Sl st into first 25 sts, ch4 (counts as 1 dc, ch 1), skip st at base of ch 4 and next st, *1dc into foll st, ch1, skip next st; rep from * until only 25 sts remain unworked (not including st just skipped), 1dc into next st, leave rem sts unworked, turn.

Row 3: Ch1, 1sc into first st, 1sc into next ch 1 space, *ch3, then a further ch7, sl st into 7th ch from hook, turn work (this makes it easier to work into the loop) and then (1sc, 1hdc, 12dc, 1hdc, 1sc) into 7ch loop, ch3, skip next (1dc, ch1, 1dc), work 1sc into next ch 1 space, [1sc into next dc and 1sc into foll ch 1 space] twice (5sc in total); rep from * to end, finishing after final (8th) roundel with ch3, 1sc into ch 4 space, 1sc into 3rd ch of ch 4, fasten off.

TO MAKE UP

Weave in ends (see page 125).
Press to make choker lie flat.

CHAPTER 5

For Children

Crochet does make it easy to embrace the super-cute factor when you're making projects for children or for the nursery. As well as cozy things to wear and blankets to snuggle up into, this chapter includes two of the most adorable toys, which are bound to become firm favorites for boys and girls alike.

CHILD'S *Cowl*

In my experience, scarves are just too tricky for kids; they either have them dragging along the ground or end up tangling themselves up. The whole point should be to keep them warm, and this cowl is just about perfect for that!

COWL

Using 2 strands (take one from the center of the ball and one from the outside) of A, ch44 loosely. Check the chain fits round your child's head; if it doesn't seem long enough add two or four more stitches, though remember it will stretch a bit. Making sure the chain is not twisted, join it with a sl st to form a ring.

Round 1: Ch1 (does not count as st), 1sc into same place, 1sc into next st and into every st to end of rnd, join with a sl st to top of first sc, do not turn. *(44 sts)*

Change to one strand each of B and C, holding both strands together.

Round 2: Ch2 (counts as 1 hdc), 1hdc into next st and into every st to end of rnd, join with a sl st to top of ch 2, do not turn.

Rounds 3–14: Rep rnd 2.

Fasten off B and C, and join in 2 strands of A.

Round 15: Ch1, 1sc into same place, 1sc into next st and into every st to end of rnd, join with a sl st to top of ch 2, fasten off.

TO MAKE UP

Weave in ends (see page 125).

Yarn

Debbie Bliss Rialto Aran (100% merino wool) worsted-weight (Aran) yarn, 1¾oz (50g), 85yd (78m) balls

Small amount of Rose 16 (A)

2 balls in Gold 7 (B)

2 balls in Ecru 2 (C)

Hook and equipment

US K/10½ (7mm) crochet hook

Large tapestry needle

Size

21¾in (55cm) circumference and 8¾in (22cm) deep

Gauge

8 hdc and 7 rows over 4in (10cm) using US K/10½ (7mm) crochet hook

Abbreviations

See page 114

CHILD'S *Beanie*

This lovely child's hat has a matching cowl (see page 92). It is a great, easy project suitable for a beginner, and creates a lovely gift very, very quickly! The beanie is exactly what you want from a child's hat—simple, fun, warm, and easy to spot in a crowd! Both projects use the same yarn, which is two colors held together; this gives a lovely marl effect where the colors randomly twist around each other. You do not need to wind the two colors into one ball before using the yarn, simply hold one strand from each separate ball at the same time.

Yarn

Debbie Bliss Rialto Aran (100% merino wool) worsted-weight (Aran) yarn, 1¾oz (50g), 85yd (78m) balls

2 balls in Rose 16 (A)

2 balls in Gold 7 (B)

2 balls in Ecru 2 (C)

Hook and equipment

US K/10½ (7mm) crochet hook

Large tapestry needle

Size

20in (50cm) circumference and 7½in (19cm) from top to rim

Gauge

8 hdc and 7 rows over 4in (10cm) using US K/10½ (7mm) crochet hook

Abbreviations

See page 114

HAT

Using A and B together, ch4, join with a sl st to form a ring.

Round 1: Ch2 (counts as 1 hdc), work 9hdc into the ring, join with a sl st to top of ch 2, do not turn. *(10 sts)*

Round 2: Ch2 (counts as 1 hdc), 1hdc into same st (at base of ch 2), 2hdc into next st (this is quite difficult to see as it looks very close to the ch 2), 2hdc into each st to end of rnd, join with a sl st to top of ch 2, do not turn. *(20 sts)*

Round 3: Ch2 (counts as 1 hdc), 1hdc into same st, 1hdc into next st, *2hdc into foll st, 1hdc into next st; rep from * to end of rnd, finishing with 1hdc in last st, join with a sl st to top of ch 2, do not turn. *(30 sts)*

Round 4: Ch2 (counts as 1 hdc) 1hdc into same st, *1hdc into each of next two sts, 2hdc into foll st; rep from * to end of rnd, finishing with 1hdc into each of last 2 sts, join with a sl st to top of ch 2, do not turn. *(40 sts)*

Round 5: Ch2 (counts as 1 hdc), 1hdc into foll st and into every st to end of rnd, join with a sl st to top of ch 2, do not turn. *(40 sts)*

Rounds 6–13: Rep rnd 5. You can make the hat larger or smaller here, just keep trying it on for size.

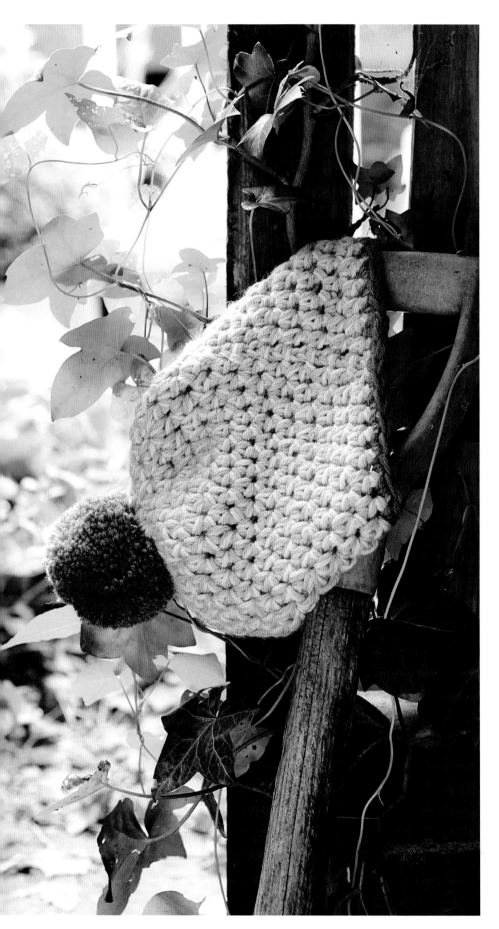

Fasten off A and B and join in 2 strands of C (take one from the center of the ball and one from the outside) at the back of the hat.

Round 14 (trim): Ch1, 1sc into same place, 1 sc into every st to end of rnd, join with a sl st to first sc made, fasten off.

TO MAKE UP
Weave in ends (see page 125).

POMPOM
Make a fabulous pompom using C. Keep ends quite long after you have tied it and use these to attach the pompom to the hat.

Colors
If you do not want to do a contrast pompom and trim, you should have enough of the main colors to just use these instead.

DEEP CHEVRON *Baby blanket*

Ripples and chevrons are the mainstay of crochet and this lovely baby blanket is a great twist on a classic chevron. I should say that it is little more complicated than the standard chevron, so if you are a beginner to crochet it is probably worth learning the basic stitch first (see page 111). However, as with all crochet, once you've got started you should find it easy to keep going. There is a chart as well as written instructions to help you work this stitch pattern.

Yarn

Blue Sky Fibers Worsted Cotton (100% organic cotton) worsted-weight (Aran) yarn, 3½oz (100g), 150yd (137m) skeins

1 skein in Sleet 635 (A)
1 skein in Drift 614 (B)
1 skein in Shell 606 (C)
1 skein in Pink Parfait 642 (D)
1 skein in Lotus 617 (E)

Hook and equipment

US G/6 or H/8 (4.5mm) crochet hook
Large tapestry needle

Size

31 ½ x 26¼in (80 x 67cm)

Gauge

1 pattern rep (20 sts and 6 rows) over 4in (10cm) using US G/6 or H/8 (4.5mm) crochet hook

Abbreviations

Group = 1dc, ch1, 1dc worked into same space.
See also page 114

BLANKET

Using A, ch143 loosely. (The stitch patt is a multiple of 20 +3 if you want to make the blanket larger or smaller.)

Row 1: 1dc into 5th ch from hook, ch1, 1dc into same space, *ch1, skip 3 ch, (1dc, ch1, 1dc) into next ch, ch1, skip 3 ch, (1dc, ch1, 1dc, ch3, 1dc, ch1, 1dc) into next ch, ch1, skip 3 ch, (1dc, ch1, 1dc) into next ch, ch1, skip 3 ch, **(1dc, ch1, 1dc) into next ch, do not ch1, skip 3 ch, (1dc, ch1, 1dc) into next ch; rep from * to last 3 ch, you should be at ** in the patt, (1dc, ch1, 1dc) into 3rd ch from end, skip 1 ch, 1dc into last ch, turn.

Row 2: Ch3 (counts as 1dc), skip first group from row 1, (1dc, ch1, 1dc) into first ch 1 space between last two groups of row 1, *ch1, skip next group, (1dc, ch1, 1dc) into next ch 1 space between groups, ch1, (1dc, ch1, 1dc, ch3, 1dc, ch1, 1dc) into ch 3 space, ch1, skip next group from row 1, work (1dc, ch1, 1dc) into next ch 1 space between groups, ch1, skip next group from row 1, work (1dc, ch1, 1dc) into next ch 1 space, **do not ch1, skip the decrease group from row 1, (1dc, ch1, 1dc) into next ch 1 space; rep from * to ch 1 space before final group, you should be ** in the patt, do not ch1, work 1dc into top of turning ch from row 1. Fasten off A, turn.

PATTERN REPEAT

Row 3 and every row thereafter is essentially a repeat of row 2, however, there are two main differences.

1: All stitches, apart from the increase group, are worked into the stitches 2 rows below (row 1 when working row 3). The increase group is worked as normal into the ch 3 space in the row below (row 2 when working row 3).

2: The (1dc, ch1, 1dc) groups are now worked into the ch 1 space within each group (from 2 rows below), NOT into the ch 1 space between groups.

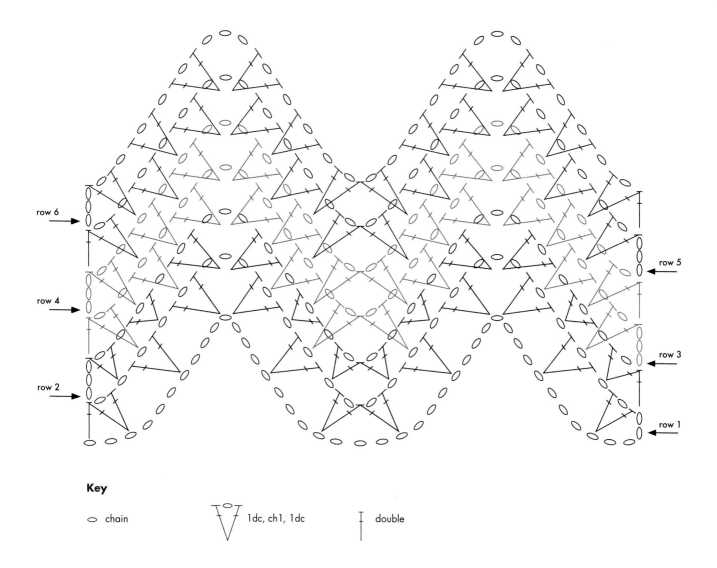

row 6
row 4
row 2
row 5
row 3
row 1

Key

◯ chain

⋁ 1dc, ch1, 1dc

⊺ double

Make a rainbow

I've chosen a fairly muted palette, but you could go wild with the colors! If you don't know the sex of the baby then a rainbow is always fabulous, and the Blue Sky yarn colors are perfect for this. Working into two rows below means that the colors run into each other beautifully, so be brave!

Row 3: Join B, ch3 (counts as 1 dc), skip first group from row 1 and ch 1 space, work a group in ch 1 space within second group, *ch1, work another group into next group from row 1, ch1, (1dc, ch1, 1dc, ch3, 1dc, ch1, 1dc) into ch 3 space from row 2, ch1, work a group into next group from row 1, ch1, work a group into next group, **do not ch1, skip decrease group from row 1, work a group into foll group in row 1; rep from *, you should finish at ** in second-to-last group from row 1, do not ch1, skip final group, 1dc into top of ch 3, turn.

Rep row 3, changing color every two rows until 40 rows have been worked in total. Then rep row 3, 5 times more and changing color on every row to make a single-row striped band across the top of the blanket. Remember to work all stitches in the spaces from two rows below, apart for the increase; so for row 4 you are working into row 2, and so on.

TO MAKE UP

Weave in ends (see page 125).
Press blanket following instructions on ball band.

BABY *Cardigan*

There is something so special about crafting a cardigan for a new baby, not just because you are creating a unique item for a new life, but also because you can use luxury yarns to make your cardigan super-gorgeous. This cardi based on a very traditional design: it starts at the top and gradually increases over the bobble yoke section before you split off the sleeves. There is nothing tricky at all about the pattern, so please do have a go even if you've never tried making a garment before.

Yarn

Blue Sky Fibers Baby Alpaca (100% baby alpaca) sport-weight (baby) yarn, 1¾oz (50g), 110yd (100m) skeins
  2 skeins in Natural White 500 (A)
  1 skein in Petal Pink 516 (B)

Other materials

3 x buttons ⅝in (1.5cm) in diameter

Hook and equipment

US F/5 (3.75mm) crochet hook
Large tapestry needle

Size

To fit: 3-6(6-9:9-12) months
Finished measurements
Chest: 18½(20½:23¾in (42(52:60)cm)
Length (nape to hem): 8¾(9:9½)in (22(23:24)cm)

Gauge

18 dc sts and 9 dc rows over 4in (10cm) using US F/5 (3.75mm) crochet hook

Abbreviations

BOBBLE = hdc3tog in same space, yoh and pull through to secure.
See also page 114

CARDIGAN

Cardigan is made from the top down in one piece.
Using A, ch46(50:56) loosely.
Row 1: Work 1sc into 2nd ch from hook and into every ch to end, turn. *(45(49:55) sts)*
Row 2: Ch1, 1sc into same place, 1sc into every st to end, fasten off A, turn.
Row 3: Join in B, ch3 (counts as 1 hdc, ch 1), skip st at the base of ch 2 and foll st, *BOBBLE into next st, ch1, skip next st; rep from * to end of row, finishing after final bobble with ch1, skip 1 st, 1hdc into last st, fasten off B. *(21(23:26) bobbles)*
Row 4: Join in A, ch1, 1sc into same place, *2sc into ch 1 space, 1sc into top of next bobble; rep from * to end of rnd, finishing with 1sc into final bobble, 2sc into ch 3 space, 1sc into 2nd ch of ch 3, turn. *(67(73:82) sts)*
Row 5: Ch3 (counts as 1 dc), skip st at base of ch 3, 1dc into foll st and into each st to end of row.
Small(medium)
Row 6: Ch1, 1sc into same place, 1sc into every st to end of row, turn. *(67(73) sts)*
Large
Row 6: As for small(medium), except in or around the center of the back work 2sc into 1 st to increase the stitch count by 1. *(83 sts)*

Choosing yarn

Blue Sky Fibers Baby Alpaca yarn is divine. With a gorgeous squishiness and high sheen, it creates a beautiful stitch definition in the finished cardigan.

All sizes cont

Row 7: Rep row 3. *(32(35:40) bobbles)*

Row 8: Rep row 4. *(100(109:124) sts)*

Row 9: Rep row 5.

Medium

Row 10: Ch1, 1sc into same place, 1sc into every st to end of row, turn. *(101(109) sts)*

Small(large)

Row 10: As for medium, except in or around the center of the back work 2sc into 1 st to increase the stitch count by 1. *(101(125) sts)*

All sizes cont

Row 11: Rep row 3. *(49(53:61) bobbles)*

Medium(large)

Row 12: Join in A, ch1, 1sc into same place, *2sc into ch 1 space, 1sc into top of next bobble, 1sc into next ch 1 space, 1sc into top of foll bobble; rep from * to end of row. *(136(156) sts)*

Small

Row 12: As for medium(large), except in the center of the back in one pattern rep only, work 1sc into ch 1 space in place of 2sc, this will give an odd number of stitches at end of row, turn. *(125 sts)*

All sizes cont

Row 13: Rep row 5.

Small

Row 14: Ch1, 1sc into same place, 1sc into every st to end of row, turn. *(125(137) sts)*

Medium(large)

Row 14: As for small(medium), except in or around the center of the back work 2sc into 1 st to increase the stitch count by 1. *(137(157) sts)*

Row 15: Rep row 3. *(61(67:77) bobbles)*

Row 16: Ch1, 1sc into same place, *2sc into ch 1 space, 1sc into top of next bobble, 1sc into next ch 1 space, 1sc into top of foll bobble; rep from * to end of row.

Row 17: Rep row 5. *(156(171:196) sts)*

DIVIDE FOR THE BODY AND SLEEVES

BODY

Row 1: Ch1, 1sc into same place and 1sc into each of foll 20(22:25) sts, skip next 35(38:44) sts (this will be worked later and is first sleeve), 1sc into each of next 44(49:56) sts, skip foll 35(38:44) sts (second sleeve), 1sc into each of final 21(23:26) sts (the ch 3 counts as last st), turn. *(86(95:108) sts)*

Small(large)

Row 2: Ch3 (counts as 1 dc), skip st at base of ch 3, 1dc into next st and into every st to reach approx. the middle st, 2dc in this st, then cont working 1dc into every st to end of row, turn. *(87(109) sts)*

Medium

Row 2: Ch3 (counts as 1 dc), skip st at base of ch 3, 1dc into next st and into every st to end of row, turn. *(95 sts)*

All sizes cont

Row 3: Ch3 (counts as 1 dc), skip st at base of ch 3, 1dc into next st and into every st to end of row, turn.

Rep row 3, 4(5:6) more times.

Next row: Ch1, 1sc into same place, 1sc into every st, to end of row, turn.

Next row: Ch3 (counts as 1 hdc, ch 1), skip st at the base of ch 2 and foll st, *BOBBLE into next st, ch1, skip next st; rep from * to end of row, finishing after final bobble with ch1, skip 1 st, 1hdc into last st.

Next row: Ch1, 1sc into same place, *1sc into next ch 1 space, 1sc into top of foll bobble; rep from * to end of row, turn.

Next row: Ch3 (counts as 1 dc), skip st at base of ch 3, 1dc into next st and into every st to end of row, turn.

Next row: Ch1, 1sc into same place, 1sc into next st and into every st to end of row, fasten off.

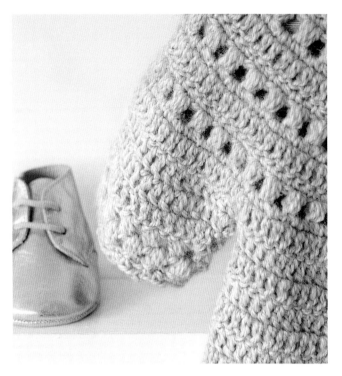

Round 2: Ch3 (counts as 1 dc), dc2tog over next 2 sts, 1dc into next st and into every st to last 2 sts, dc2tog, join with a sl st to top of ch 3, turn. *(33(36:42) sts)*

Round 3: Rep rnd 2, fasten off if working small size. *(31(34:40) sts)*

For medium and large sizes, rep round 1, 1(2) more times, fasten off.

Round 4: Join in B at the underarm, ch2, hdc2tog into same place as ch2, yoh, *ch1, skip 1 st, bobble into next st; rep from * to end of rnd, skipping 2 sts at end of rnd for the SMALL size, join with a sl st to top of first bobble, do not turn.

Round 5: Sl st into next ch 1 space, ch2, hdc2tog in this ch 1 space, *ch1, BOBBLE into next ch 1 space; rep from * to end of rnd, join with a sl st to top of first bobble, fasten off B.

Round 6: Join in A, ch1, 1 sc into same place, work 1 sc into every bobble and ch sp to end of rnd, join with a sl st to first sc, do not turn.

Round 7: Ch1, 1sc into same place, 1sc into next st, *ch3, sl st into 3rd ch from hook (picot made), skip next st, 1sc into each of foll 2 sts; rep from * to end of rnd, join with a sl st to first sc made, fasten off.

Rep for second sleeve.

TO MAKE UP

Weave in ends (see page 125).
Sew the buttons to the button band.

BUTTONHOLE BAND

Row 1: Join A to the bottom of RH side, work a row of sc evenly up the RH edge, (as a general rule working 2sc along the side of every dc and 1sc in every sc and hdc).

Row 2: As row 1, but at row of doubles between bobble row 3 and 7, ch2, skip 1 st (first buttonhole made), cont working 1sc into every st to dc row between bobble row 7 and 11, ch2, skip 1 st (second buttonhole made), cont working 1sc into every st to dc row between bobble rows 11 and 15, ch2, skip 1 st (third buttonhole made), then cont working 1sc into every st to the bottom, turn.

Row 3: Work 1sc into every st to end of row, fasten off.

BUTTON BAND

Row 1: Join A to the top of LH side, work a row of sc evenly down the LH edge, (as a general rule working 2sc along the side of every dc and 1sc in every sc and hdc).

Rows 2–3: Work 1sc into every st to end of row.
Fasten off.

SLEEVE

Rejoin the yarn at the underarm of one sleeve with the RS facing.

Round 1: Ch3 (counts as 1 dc), skip st at the base of ch 3, 1dc into next st and into every st to end of rnd, join with a sl st to top of ch 3, turn. *35(38:44 sts)*

Be careful not to work into the stitches that you have already worked in the body, this is very easy to do, so it is probably best to count if in doubt!

TIGER *Toy*

More of a Tigger than a scary Tiger, I love the way this gorgeous feline can give you a cuddle with his squidgy arms, and sit by you or on you with his little legs dangling beneath him! Rather like the owl (see page 108), this toy is crocheted from the bottom up in the round. The head is separate and all his appendages are added once his body and head are stuffed. So when you come to create his features, you can experiment with placing the eyes and muzzle to get them just right, and add your own personal touches.

Yarn

Mrs Moon Plump (80% superfine merino wool, 20% baby alpaca) super-bulky (super-chunky) yarn, 3½oz (100g), 76yd (70m) skeins
  2 skeins in Earl Grey (A)
  2 skeins in Marmalade (B)
  Small amount of Pavlova (C)

Other materials

Toy stuffing

Hook and equipment

US L/11 (8mm) crochet hook
Large tapestry needle

Size

14½in (37cm) high when sitting

Gauge

7 dc sts and 4 dc rows over 4in (10cm) using US L/11 (8mm) crochet hook

Abbreviations

See page 114

BODY

Note that you need to start stuffing the body as you start to decrease. Do not fasten off yarn between rows but carry it up on the inside of the body.
Using A, ch4, join with a sl st to form a ring.
Round 1: Ch3 (counts as 1 dc), work 11 dc into the ring, join with sl st to top of ch 3. *(12 dc)*
Round 2: Join in B, ch3 (counts as 1 dc), 1dc into same place, 2dc into next dc and into every dc to end of rnd, join rnd with sl st to top of ch 3, do not turn. *(24 sts)*
Round 3: Change to A, ch3 (counts as 1 dc), 1dc into same place, *1dc into foll st, 2dc into next st; rep from * to end of rnd, finish with 1dc in last st, join with a sl st to top of ch 3, do not turn. *(36 sts)*
Round 4: Using B and working in BLO, ch3 (counts as 1 dc), 1dc into next st and into every st to end of rnd, join rnd with a sl st to top of ch 3, do not turn.
Round 5: Using A, ch3 (counts as 1 dc), 1dc into next st and into every st to end of rnd, join rnd with a sl st to top of ch 3, do not turn.
Rounds 6–13: Rep rnd 5, changing color every row.
Round 14: Using A, ch3 (counts as 1 dc), 1dc into next st, dc2tog, *1dc into each of next 2 sts, dc2tog; rep from * to end of rnd, join with a sl st to top of ch 3, do not turn. *(27 sts)*
Round 15: Using B, ch3 (counts as 1 dc), dc2tog, *1dc into foll st, dc2tog; rep from * to end of rnd, join with a sl st to top of ch 3, do not turn. *(18 sts)*
Round 16: Using A, ch3 (counts as 1 dc), dc2tog, dc2tog; rep from * to last st, 1dc in last st, join with a sl st to top of ch 3, do not turn.
Round 17: Using B, rep rnd 16.
Make sure body is nicely stuffed and fasten off.

HEAD

Note that you need to stuff the head as you work it.
Do not fasten off yarn between rows but bring it up on the inside of the head.
Using A, ch4, join with a sl st to form a ring.
Round 1: Ch3, (counts as 1 dc), 11 dc into ring, join with a sl st to top of ch 3, do not turn. *(12 sts)*

Round 2: Using B, ch3 (counts as 1 dc), 1dc into same place, 2dc into every st to end of rnd, join with a sl st to top of ch 3, do not turn. *(24 sts)*

Round 3: Using A, ch3 (counts as 1 dc), 1 dc into same place, *1dc into each of next 2 sts, 2dc into foll st; rep from * finishing with 1 dc into each of last 2 sts, join with a sl st to top of ch 3, do not turn. *(32 sts)*

Round 4: Using B, ch3 (counts as 1 dc), 1dc into next st and into every st to end of rnd, join with a sl st to top of ch 3, do not turn.

Rounds 5–8: Rep rnd 4, changing color every row.

Round 9: Using A, ch2 (counts as 1 hdc), 1hdc into next st, hdc2tog, *1hdc into each of next 2 sts, hdc2tog; rep from * finishing with hdc2tog, join with a sl st to top of ch 2, do not turn. *(24 sts)*

Round 10: Using B, ch2 (counts as 1 hdc), hdc2tog, *1 hdc into next st, hdc2tog; rep from * finishing with hdc2tog, join with sl st to top of ch 2, do not turn. *(16 sts)*

Round 11: Using A, ch2 (counts as 1 hdc), hdc2tog over next 2 sts, cont working hdc2tog to end of rnd, finish with 1hdc, join rnd with a sl st to top of ch 2, do not turn. *(9 sts)*

Round 12: Using B, ch2 (counts as 1 hdc), hdc2tog over next 2 sts, cont working hdc2tog, to end of rnd, finish with 1hdc, join rnd with a sl st to top of ch 2, fasten off.

LEG AND FOOT

(Make 2)

Using C, ch2.

Round 1: 8sc into 2nd ch from hook, join with a sl st to first sc made, do not turn. You may want to mark the first sc as it is not that easy to see! *(8 sts)*

Round 2: Ch1, 2sc into same place, 2sc into every st to end of rnd, join with a sl st to top of first sc made, fasten off. *(16 sts)*

Round 3: Join in B, ch1, 1sc into same place, 1sc into next st and into every st to end of rnd, join with a sl st to first sc made, do not turn. *(16 sc)*

Round 4: Rep rnd 3.

Round 5: Join in A, ch1, 1sc into same place, 1sc into next st, *sc2tog over next 2 sts, 1sc into each of foll 2 sts; rep from * to last 2 sts, sc2tog, join with a sl st to top of first sc made, do not turn. *(12 sts)*

Round 6: Rep rnd 5. *(9 sts)*

Round 7: Using B, ch1, 1sc into same place, 1sc into next st and into every st to end of rnd, join with a sl st to top of first sc made, do not turn. *(9 sts)*

Round 8: Rep rnd 7.

Fasten off.

Stuff each leg. The ends remain open.

ARM

(Make 2)

Using C, ch2.

Round 1: 8sc into the 2nd ch from hook, join with a sl st to first sc made, fasten off. *(8 sts)*

Round 2: Join in B, ch1, 1sc into same place, 1sc into next st

and into every st to end of rnd, join with a sl st to top of first sc made, do not turn. *(8 sts)*

Rounds 3–17: Rep rnd 2, changing color every 2 rnds. Stuff the arms as you go. The ends remain open.

MUZZLE

Using C, ch4.

Round 1: (3tr, 3dc, ch1, 1tr, ch1, 3dc, 3tr, ch2) all into 4th ch from hook, sl st into center of muzzle, you should end up with a heart shape, fasten off.

NOSE

Using A, ch4.

Round 1: 1sc into 2nd and 3rd ch from hook, sl st into 4th ch, turn and work down the other side of the chain by sl st into what was the 4th ch again, 1sc into each of next 2 ch, 1 sl st into final ch, pull tight (should look like a triangle), fasten off.

EYE

(Make 2)

Using C, ch2.

Round 1: Work 8sc into the 2nd ch from hook, pull tight, and fasten off. Using A, embroider a pupil.

EAR

(Make 2)

Using C, ch4.

Round 1: 1sc into 2nd and 3rd ch from hook, sl st into 4th ch, turn and work down the other side of the chain by sl st into what was the 4th ch again, 1sc into each of next 2 ch, 1 sl st into final ch, pull tight (should look like a triangle), fasten off.

Round 2: Join in B, ch1, 1sc into same place, work 1 sc into next st, 3sc into end st, turn, work 1sc into each of next 2 sts.

Round 3: Join in A, ch1, 1sc into same place, 1sc into each of next 2 sts, 1sc into next st, ch3, 1sc into next st and into each of the final 2 sts, fasten off.

TAIL

Work as for arm, but work 25 rounds in total.

TO MAKE UP

Weave in ends on all parts (see page 125).

Sew head onto the body. Then sew on the legs, arms, and tail using the photo as a guide. Sew the facial features and sew a line up from the bottom of the muzzle to the nose.

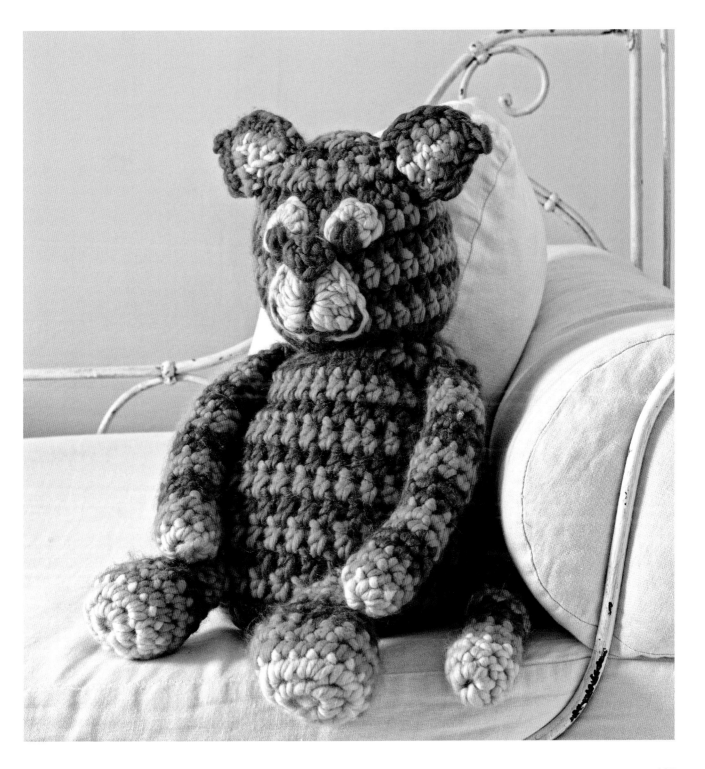

GRANNY RECTANGLE *Bolero*

This is a great first garment project for someone new to crochet, and is totally adorable! It's perfect to keep a little girl warm when she's wearing her favorite party dress, and unlike most cardigans, it adds something really special rather than detracting from the main event. You can make it as big or small as you want by just adding or taking away rounds. Also, of course, you can jazz up or down the color combinations—I think that a plain color would look lovely, too!

Yarn

Mrs Moon Plump DK (80% superfine merino wool, 20% baby alpaca) light-worsted-weight (double knitting) yarn, 1¾oz (50g), 125yd (115m) skeins
  1 skein in Fondant Fancy (A)
  1 skein in Rhubarb Crumble (B)
Mrs Moon Fluff (80% kid mohair, 20% silk) fingering (lace weight) yarn, ¾oz (25g), 218yd (200m) skeins
1 ball in Rhubarb Crumble (C)

Hook and equipment

US G/6 or H/8 (4.5mm) crochet hook
Large tapestry needle

Size

To fit: 5-6(6-7:7-8) years
Finished measurements
Width (before seaming): 15(17¼:18¾)in (38(44:48)cm)
Length (nape to hem): 11(13½:15)in (28(34:38)cm)

Gauge

4 groups of 3 dc sts (including 4 ch spaces) and 9 rows over 4in (10cm) using US G/6 or H/8 (4.5mm) crochet hook

Abbreviations

See page 114

RECTANGLE

Using A, ch18.

Round 1: 1dc into 4th ch from hook, 1dc into next ch, *ch1, skip 1 ch, 1dc into each of next 3 ch; rep from * twice more, ch2, 3dc into last ch, ch2 (you are now moving round to the other side of the foundation chain), 1dc into each of next 3 ch (these already have doubles in on the side you have just completed), **ch1, skip 1 ch, 1dc into each of next 3 ch; rep from ** twice more, (you should now be working in the st at the base of ch 3), ch2, 3dc into same st, ch2, join the rnd with a sl st to top of ch 3, do not turn.

Round 2: Sl st into each of next two dc and into ch 1 space, ch3 (counts as 1 dc), 2dc into same ch 1 space, (ch1, 3dc) into next two ch 1 spaces, ch1, (3dc, ch2, 3dc) into ch 2 space, ch1, (3dc, ch2, 3dc) into foll ch 2 space, *ch1, 3dc into next ch 1 space; rep from * twice more, ch1, (3dc, ch2, 3dc) into next ch 2 space, ch1, (3dc, ch2, 3dc) into final ch 2 space, ch1, join with a sl st to top of ch 3, fasten off A, do not turn.

Round 3: Join B to top right ch 2 corner space, ch3 (counts as 1 dc), (2dc, ch2, 3dc) into same ch 2 space, (ch1, 3dc) into next four ch 1 spaces, *ch1, (3dc, ch2, 3dc) into ch 2 space, ch1, 3dc into next ch 1 space; rep from * once more, (ch1, 3dc) into next three ch 1 spaces, ch1, (3dc, ch2, 3dc) into last corner ch 2 space, ch1, 3dc into last ch 1 space, join with a sl st to top of ch 3, do not turn.

Rounds 4–13: Rep rnd 3, changing color every 2 rnds, beginning with 2 rnds of A. Work (3dc, ch2, 3dc) into every ch 2 corner space and 3dc into every ch 1 side space, all groups of dc must be separated by ch 1 (except the ch 2 in each corner).

When starting a new round but keeping same color, always slip stitch over next 2 dc and into next space as every round must start in a space. Ch3 at start of all new rounds and that ch 3 counts as 1 dc.

6–7 years (7–8 years)

Work 2(4) more rnds.

Alternatively measure the bolero against the child and increase as necessary.

TO MAKE UP

Weave in ends (see page 125).

Sew up the bolero by folding it in half lengthways, then put a couple of stitches in last dc on either end of the long end.

TRIM

Round 1: Using C, work one complete round of sc around the inside edge and each sleeve edge, working 1sc into every dc and 1sc into every ch1 space.

Round 2 (picot): Work around inside edge and both sleeve edges alike, join C to any sc from rnd 1, ch1, 1sc into same place, 1sc into each of next two sts, *ch3, sl st into 3rd ch from hook (picot made), 1sc into each of next 3 sts; rep from * to end of rnd, join with a sl st to first sc, fasten off.

GIANT *Cuddly owl*

Warning: this owl is so cute, you won't want to give him away.... bear this in mind before you start making him! He is a very simple construction, crocheted from the bottom up in the round, and then the crown, eyes, ears, wings, and feet are added afterward. The simple stitches give him a texture and look that is totally adorable! When it comes to stuffing the owl, I've gone for a very soft, squidgy feel making him perfect for a child, but you can do as you please: you can even weight him and use him as a doorstop. Personally though, I think he is best for cuddling—squashy and soft and very, very cute!

Yarn

Mrs Moon Plump (80% superfine merino wool, 20% baby alpaca) super-bulky (super-chunky) yarn, 3½oz (100g), 76yd (70m) skeins

  3 skeins in Earl Grey (A)

  3 skeins in Pavlova (B)

  Small amount of Marmalade (feet and beak) (C)

Mrs Moon Plump DK (80% superfine merino wool, 20% baby alpaca) light-worsted-weight (double knitting) yarn, 1¾oz (50g), 125yd (115m) skeins

Small amounts of Pavlova, Marmalade, and Earl Grey for the eyes

Other materials

Toy stuffing

Hooks and equipment

US L/11 (8mm) crochet hook and US O/17 (12mm) crochet hooks
Large tapestry needle

Size

12in (30cm) high, 42½in (108cm) circumference

Gauge

9 sc sts and 10 sc rows over 4in (10cm) using US L/11 (8mm) crochet hook

Abbreviations

PUFF = hdc3tog in same space, yoh and pull through to secure.
PUFF1 = This is worked at the beginning of the rnd to incorporate the turning ch: hdc2tog in same space, yoh and pull through to secure.
See also page 114

BODY

Using 8mm (US L/11) hook and A, ch6, join with a sl st to form a ring.
Round 1: Ch3 (counts as 1 dc), work 15dc into ring. *(16 dc)*
Round 2: Ch3 (counts as 1 dc), 1dc into same place, 2dc into each dc, join with a sl st to top of ch 3. *(32 sts)*
Round 3: Ch3 (counts as 1 dc), 1dc into same place, 1dc into next st, *2dc into next st, 1dc into next st; rep from * to end, join with a sl st to top of ch 3. *(48 sts)*

Round 4: Ch3 (counts as 1 dc), 1dc into same place, 1dc into each of next 2 sts, *2dc into next st, 1dc into each of next 2 sts; rep from * to end, join with a sl st to top of ch 3. *(64 sts)*
Round 5: Ch 3 (counts as 1 dc), 1dc into same place, 1dc into each of next 3 dc, *2dc into next st, 1dc into each of next 3 dc; rep from * to end, join with a sl st to top of ch 3. *(80 sts: base of owl complete)*
Note you must weave in any ends on the inside of the owl as you crochet, and you will also need to start stuffing him as he grows.

Round 6: Ch1, sc2tog (working 1st sc of sc2tog into same st as ch1), 1sc into each of next 38 sts, sc2tog, 1sc in every st to end of rnd, join with sl st. *(78 sts)*

Round 7: Ch3 (counts as 1 dc), 2dc into same place, *skip 2 sc, 1 sc into next st, skip 2 sc, 5dc into next st; rep from * to end, finishing with 2dc into st at base of ch 3, then to complete the 5dc group join with sl st to top of ch 3. Do not fasten off, but carry yarn A up the inside for rnd 9. *(13 shells)*

Round 8: Join B to where you left off in the previous rnd, ch1, 1sc into same place (middle dc of 5dc), *skip 2 dc, 5dc in next sc, skip 2 dc, 1sc into next dc; rep from * to end of rnd, finishing with 5dc in last sc, join with a sl st to 1st sc. Do not fasten off, but carry yarn B up the inside for rnd 10.

Round 9: Pick up A, ch3, 2dc into same place, *1sc into 3rd dc of next shell, 5dc into next sc; rep from * to end, finishing by working 2dc into same place as first 3 dc, join with sl st to top of ch 3.
Rep rnds 8–9 until 17 rnds of shells are completed.

SHAPE TOP OF BODY

A note on decreasing: A shell decrease starts at the top of the shell (from the previous row), on the sc as folls: 1sc into 3rd dc of shell, sc into next sc, sc into 3rd dc next of shell, now work a normal shell into next sc (1 shell decreased). You always need to start a decrease on the sc at the top of a shell, so if you are not in this place at the end of a rnd, you must sl st into the first 3 dc of next shell and then work the decrease.

Finish stuffing the owl as you decrease rows.

Round 18: You should be on a B rnd; starting with a sc at the top of a shell, ch1, *1sc into same place, 1sc into next sc, 1sc into the middle dc of next shell, work 2 normal shells, then one shell decrease; rep from *—so working one shell decrease followed by two normal shells—finish with a decrease, then join rnd with a sl st to top of first sc made. *(8 shells, 5 decreases: note that it really doesn't matter how neat this looks as long as it is reasonably even as it will be covered by the ears/top.)*

Round 19: Change to A, *sc3tog, work one shell decrease, work 1 normal shell; rep from * to end, finishing with sc3tog, join rnd with a sl st to top of 1st sc3tog.

Round 20: Cont in A, ch1, then cont to decrease by working dc2togs and working 1 sc in top of remaining shells to decrease them. Do not sl st to join but cont to work in a spiral, working dc2togs until top is covered. Switch to sc2togs in final rnds if necessary to close hole.

Fasten off and weave in ends.

EARS/TOP

Using US L/11 (8mm) hook and B, ch22.

Row 1: Work 1 sc into 2nd ch from hook and in every ch to end of row, turn.

Row 2: Ch1, 1sc into same place and into every st to end of row, turn.

Rep row 2, 21 times more, or until work is square.

Fasten off.

EDGING/EARS

Join in A, ch1, 1sc into same place, 1sc into next st and into every st to last st, in last st of this row work the first ear as folls: ch3, sl st into the corner, ch5, sl st into the corner, ch3, sl st into next st, cont working a row of sc evenly along the edge, 3sc into next corner, and work sc evenly along bottom edge, work another ear into next corner, work a row of sc evenly along the final edge, 3sc into corner, fasten off yarn, and weave in ends. Position this piece onto the top of the owl's head with the ears either side of the center and sew in place, pinching the ears and sewing across the base of them, but leaving the picot edges sticking out (see photograph).

EYE

(Make 2)

Using US L/11 (8mm) hook and Plump DK throughout, using Earl Grey, ch5 and join with a sl st to form a ring, being careful not to twist the chain.

Round 1: Ch3 (counts as 1 dc), work 15 more dc into the ring, join rnd to top of ch 3 with a sl st, fasten off A. *(16 sts)*

Round 2: Join Marmalade to any dc, ch2, PUFF1 into same place, PUFF into next dc and into every dc to end of rnd, join with a sl st to top of the PUFF1, fasten off Marmalade. *(16 Puffs)*

Round 3: Join Pavlova to any space between the PUFFs, ch3 (counts as 1 dc), dc3tog, ch1, *dc4tog into next space, ch1; rep from * to end of rnd, finishing with a sl st into top of dc3tog, fasten off.

BEAK

Using C, ch8.

Row 1: 1sc into 2nd ch from hook, sc into each ch to end of row. *(7 sts)*

Row 2: Sc2tog, 1sc into each of next 3 sts, sc2tog, turn. *(5 sts)*

Row 3: Sc2tog, 1sc into next st, sc2tog, turn. *(3 sts)*

Row 4: Sc3tog, fasten off.

WING

(Make 2)

Using US O/17 (12mm) hook and one strand each of A and B held together, ch10.

Row 1: 1sc into 5th ch from hook, ch5, 1sc into the foll ch, *ch5, 1sc into next ch; rep from * to end of row, fasten off.

FOOT

(Make 2)

Using C, ch4.

Row 1: Sl st into 2nd ch from hook, then into each of next 2 ch, ch3, *sl st into 2nd and 3rd ch from hook and then into first ch made (of the ch 4), ch3; rep from * once more, fasten off.

TO MAKE UP

Weave in ends (see page 125).

Using image as a guide, position eyes, beak, wings, and feet on your owl and sew into place.

CHILD'S RETRO *Blanket*

This is a fun and easy absolute beginner project—once you know how to make a double, you are ready to go! It is excellent in-front-of-the-television crochet, and if you change colors every two rows, as I have, it seems to grow really quickly. As well as a written pattern, there is a chart to help you work this project. You always start the next row one stitch in from the row below, either by slip stitching in one stitch or, if you are starting a new color, joining it in the second stitch. This creates a slightly staggered edge that I've disguised with a pretty border. I'd really recommend weaving the ends in as you go to avoid hours of weaving in once the blanket is (almost) finished!

Yarn

Schachenmayr Merino Extrafine 120 (100% merino wool) light-worsted-weight (double-knitting) yarn, 1¾oz (50g), 131yd (120m) balls

2 balls in Limone 175 (A)
2 balls in Teerose 136 (B)
2 balls in Clematis 148 (C)
2 balls in Lemon 1175 (D)
2 balls in Cyclam 138 (E)
2 balls in Natur 102 (F)
2 balls in Teerose 136 (G)
2 balls in Flieder 145 (H)
2 balls in Maracuja 121 (J)

Hook and equipment

US F/5 or G/6 (4mm) crochet hook
Large tapestry needle

Size

58 x 32in (147 x 81cm)

Gauge

15 sc sts and 12 sc rows over 4in (10cm) using US F/5 or G/6 (4mm) crochet hook
17 dc sts and 9 dc rows over 4in (10cm) using US F/5 or G/6 (4mm) crochet hook, measured over chevron pattern

Abbreviations

See page 114

BLANKET

Using A, ch247 loosely.

Row 1: 1dc into 4th ch from hook (first 3 ch count as 1 dc), 1dc into each of next 3 ch, 3dc into next ch (this is the increase), 1dc into each of next 5 ch, skip next 2 ch (this is the decrease), 1dc into each of next 5 ch, *3dc into next ch, 1dc into each of next 5 ch, skip next 2 ch, 1dc into each of next 5 ch; rep from * to last 6 ch, 3dc into next ch, 1dc into each of last 5 ch.

Row 2: Sl st into first and second st (this is where next row starts from), ch3 (counts as 1dc), 1dc into each of next 4 dc, *3dc into next dc (this is the middle dc of increase in previous row), 1dc into each of next 5 dc, skip next 2 dc (these are the bottom two sts of decrease in previous row), 1dc into each of next 5 dc; rep from * to last 6 dc (not including 3 ch), 3dc into next dc, 1 dc into each of last 5 dc, turn (do not work into the ch 3).

Key

- ⬯ chain
- ⊢ double
- ⬮ slip stitch

Rows 3–72: Rep row 2, changing color on this row and every following second row. When changing color on a new row, join the new yarn to the second st and ch 3; you do not need to sl st as you are where you need to be to start the row. Fasten off.

BORDER
There is yarn left over to do the trim in colors of your choice; I have used B and D.

Row 1: Using B, work one row of sc evenly along each edge, ensuring the final stitch count is a multiple of 3 (as a general rule work 2sc into the length of 1 dc), turn.

Row 2: *Ch5, skip 2 sc, sl st into next st; rep from * to end. Fasten off.

Row 3: Join D to first ch 5 loop, *ch5, sl st into 3rd ch from hook, ch2, 1sc into next ch 5 loop; rep from * to end. (A basic picot or shell pattern would also look lovely.)

TO MAKE UP
Weave in ends (see page 125).

Creating chevrons
Although it looks more complicated, the blanket simply involves rows of doubles with very simple increases (working three stitches into one place) and decreases (skipping two stitches). It is also very easy to see if you have gone wrong, as the increases and decreases always fall in the same place. The decreases make very attractive holes in the blanket that are a feature of a chevron as opposed to a ripple, where there are no holes at all.

Changing size

I have made this blanket wide and quite short to go over the bottom of a child's bed, but as the stitch pattern is simply a multiple of 13, it is easy to go up or down in size. Make the chain slightly looser than you require as the chevrons shrink it slightly.

Techniques

On the following pages you'll find useful crochet techniques for making the projects in this book. From the basics of holding the hook and yarn and making your first stitches, through to changing colors neatly and finishing your work beautifully, each method is illustrated and explained.

Abbreviations

[ ]	square parentheses indicate a repeat
*	asterisk indicates where to repeat from
approx.	approximately
BLO	back loop only
ch	chain
cm	centimeter(s)
cont	continue
dc	double
dc2(3)tog	double crochet 2(3) stitches together
foll(s)	follow(s)(ing)
g	gram(s)
hdc	half double crochet
hdc2(3)tog	half double crochet 2(3) stitches together
m	meter(s)
patt	pattern
rep	repeat
RS	right side of work
sc	single crochet
sc2tog	single crochet 2 stitches together
sl st	slip stitch
st(s)	stitch(es)
tch	turning chain

WS	wrong side of work
yoh	yarn over hook

Crochet stitch conversions

Crochet stitches are worked in the same way in both the USA and the UK, but the stitch names are not the same, and identical names are used for different stitches.

Below is a list of the US terms used in this book, and the equivalent UK terms.

US TERM	UK TERM
single crochet (sc)	double crochet (dc)
half double crochet (hdc)	half treble (htr)
double crochet (dc)	treble (tr)
treble (tr)	double treble (dtr)
double treble (dtr)	triple treble (trtr)
gauge	tension
skip	miss
yarn over hook (yoh)	yarn round hook (yrh)

Holding the hook

Hold the hook in a similar way to a pencil. Do not grip it hard, and keep it balanced in your hand with the shaft resting in the crook between your index finger and your thumb.

Holding the yarn

1 Hold the yarn in your left hand. Precisely how you wrap the yarn around your fingers to tension it will vary depending on what feels comfortable for you. For a looser hold, wrap the yarn over your little finger, under the two middle fingers, and then over your index finger.

2 For a tighter hold, wrap the yarn right around your little finger, then under and over the other fingers as in Step 1.

Holding the hook and yarn together

Keep your left index finger—with the yarn draped over it—held up, and grip the work between the middle finger and thumb of your left hand, holding it just below the crochet hook.

With the hook pointing upward, catch the yarn from below. Turn the hook so it faces downward and pull the new yarn loop through the stitch or the loop on the hook. As you draw the new loop through, relax the yarn on your index finger to allow the loop to stay loose. If you tense your index finger, the loop on the hook will be pulled too tight for you to draw the new loop through.

Some left-handers learn to crochet like right-handers, but others learn with everything reversed—with the hook in their left hand and the yarn in the right. Try both ways to see which is most comfortable fo you.

Making a slip knot

A slip knot is the starting point for crochet.

1 Make a loop of yarn with the tail end going under the circle. With a crochet hook, pull a loop through the circle.

2 Slip the loop along the hook and pull the tail gently to make a loose loop on the hook.

- -

Chain (ch)

A foundation chain is needed for most projects, and chains can be made within a piece of crochet fabric.

1 Wrap the yarn over the hook ready to pull it through the loop on the hook.

2 Pull the yarn through, creating a new loop on the hook. Continue in this way to create a chain of the required number of stitches.

- -

Chain ring

The starting point for most projects worked in the round.

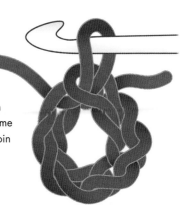

1 Make a chain the required length (see above). To join the chain into a circle, insert the crochet hook into the first chain that you made (not into the slip knot), yarn over hook.

2 Pull the yarn through the chain and through the loop on the hook at the same time, creating a slip stitch to join the chain into a circle.

Working into a stitch

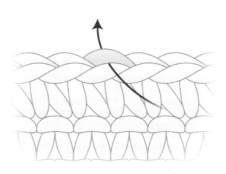

A stitch has two loops lying across the top of it. Unless otherwise directed, insert the hook under both of these loops.

Some projects in this book ask you to work into the back loop (BLO) of a stitch. To do this, insert the hook between the front and the back loop, picking up the back loop only.

Working into a chain space (ch-sp)

A chain space is the space between stitches that has been made under a chain in the previous round or row.

1 Insert the hook under the chain, not through the stitches that make it. Wrap the yarn over the hook and pull it back through the chain space.

Slip stitch (sl st)

A slip stitch doesn't create any height. It can be used to move to a different position in the work, or to join elements together.

1 Insert the hook into the work as directed, yarn over hook.

2 Pull the yarn through both the work and the loop on the hook at the same time, so that there is just one loop left on the hook.

Single crochet (sc)

1 Insert the hook into the work as directed, yarn over hook, and pull the yarn through the work only. There are two loops on the hook.

2 Yarn over hook again, and pull through the two loops on the hook, so that there is just one loop left on the hook. One single crochet stitch completed.

Making rows and rounds

When making straight rows you turn the work at the end of each row. To start the next row, you make a turning chain (tch) to create the height needed for the stitch you will use.

Single crochet = 1 chain

Half double crochet = 2 chains

Double crochet = 3 chains

When working in rounds the work is not turned, so you are always working from one side. Depending on the pattern you are working, a "round" can be square.

Start each round by making a turning chain as for working in rows. Work the required stitches to complete the round. At the end of the round, slip stitch into the top of the chain to close the round.

If you are working in a spiral, you do not need a turning chain. After completing the base ring, place a stitch marker in the first stitch and then continue to crochet around. When you have made a round and reached the point where the stitch marker is, work this stitch, take out the stitch marker from the previous round and put it back into the first stitch of the new round. A safety pin, or piece of yarn in a contrasting color, makes a good stitch marker.

Half double crochet (hdc)

1 Wrap the yarn over the hook before inserting the hook into the work as directed.

2 Yarn over hook again, and pull through the work. There are three loops on the hook.

3 Yarn over hook and pull the yarn through all three loops, so that there is just one loop left on the hook. One half double crochet stitch completed.

Double crochet (dc)

1 Wrap the yarn over the hook before inserting the hook into the work as directed. Put the hook through the work, yarn over hook again, and pull through the work. There are three loops on the hook.

2 Yarn over hook again, pull the yarn through the first two loops on the hook. There are two loops left on the hook.

3 Yarn over hook again, and pull the yarn through two loops again, so that there is just one loop left on the hook. One double crochet stitch completed.

Increasing

To increase, make two or three stitches into one stitch or space from the previous row. The illustration shows a double crochet increase being made.

Decreasing

You can decrease by either skipping the next stitch and continuing to crochet, or by crocheting two or more stitches together.

● ●

Single crochet two stitches together (sc2tog)

1 Insert the hook into the work, yarn over hook, and pull the yarn through the work so that there are two loops on the hook. Insert the hook into next stitch, yarn over hook, and pull the yarn through so that there are three loops on the hook.

2 Yarn over hook again and pull through all three loops on the hook, so that there is just one loop left on the hook. Two stitches have been worked together to decrease the number of stitches in the row by one.

● ●

Half double crochet two stitches together (hdc2tog)

1 The principle is the same as for sc2tog (see above). Make a half double stitch (see page 119) into the next stitch, but do not pull the final loop through, so there are three loops on the hook. Then repeat the process into the next stitch, so that there are five loops on the hook.

2 Yarn over hook and pull through all five loops on the hook, so that there is just one loop left on the hook. Two stitches have been worked together to decrease the number of stitches in the row by one.

● ●

Double crochet three stitches together (dc3tog)

1 To decrease double stitches, the principle is the same as for decreasing half doubles (see above). Work each double, but do not pull the final loop through. After the first double you will have two loops on the hook, and after the next double you will have three loops on the hook: for dc2tog, wrap the yarn over the hook and pull through all the loops. For dc3tog, which is the decrease illustrated here, make a final double so that there are four loops on the hook. Complete the decrease by yarn over hook and pull through all the loops, so that there is just one loop left on the hook. Three stitches have been worked together to decrease the number of stitches in the row by two.

Joining in new yarn

Whether it is a new ball of yarn, or a different color, you will have to join in yarn for all but the simplest and smallest crochet projects. The method used varies depending on where in the work the yarn needs to be joined in.

Joining into a stitch or space

The method is shown here on a stitch, but the principle is the same for joining into a chain space.

 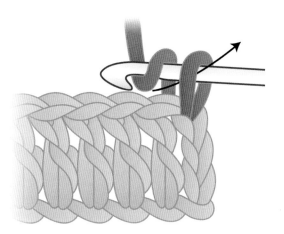

1 Make a slip knot (see page 116) and take it off the hook. Insert the hook into the stitch (or space) the yarn is to be joined to, then put the hook into the slip knot.

2 Yarn over hook, and pull through the slip knot. The yarn is securely joined in. Weave in the tail of yarn from the slip knot (see page 125) after working a row, or once the work is complete.

Joining a new color at the start of a row

1 Keep the loop of the old yarn on the hook. Drop the old yarn tail and catch the new yarn with the crochet hook.

2 Pull a loop of the new yarn through the loop on the hook, keeping the old loop drawn tight. Start crocheting with the new yarn. Weave in the tail of the old yarn (see page 125) after working a row, or once the work is complete.

Joining a new color into single crochet

For a neat color join in the middle of a row or round of single crochet, use this method.

1 Make a single crochet stitch (see page 118), but do not pull the final loop through, so there are two loops on the hook. Drop the old yarn, catch the new yarn with the hook and pull it through both loops to complete the stitch and join in the new color at the same time.

2 Continue to crochet with the new yarn. Cut the old yarn leaving a 6in (15cm) tail and weave the tail in (see page 125) after working a row, or once the work is complete.

• •

Joining a new color into double crochet

This is the method for a neat color join in the middle of a row or round of double crochet.

1 Make a double crochet stitch (see page 119), but do not pull the final loop through, so there are two loops on the hook. Drop the old yarn, catch the new yarn with the hook and pull it through both loops to complete the stitch and join in the new color at the same time.

2 Continue to crochet with the new yarn. Cut the old yarn leaving a 6in (15cm) tail and weave the tail in (see page 125) after working a row, or once the work is complete.

Seaming with single crochet

I prefer to join seams with crochet rather than sew them up. It's a quick and neat method, and easy to pull out if you make a mistake. You can use this method on the wrong side or the right side, depending on the effect you require.

1 Put the edges to be joined side by side, matching the stitches. Insert the hook under both loops of a stitch in both pieces. Wrap the yarn over the hook and pull a loop through.

2 Work a row of single crochet, inserting the hook through the stitches of both pieces each time. It's the same process as working single crochet in the usual way; just treat both pieces as a single piece.

The same principle can be used to slip stitch pieces together, working through the back loop only (see page 117). If you are looking down on an edge from above, the back loop is the loop on the outside of the edge. Insert the hook through the back loops of both pieces and slip stitch them together (see page 118).

Tassels and fringes

It is quick and easy to add a fringe to a piece of crochet.

1 Cut the length of yarn as stated in the pattern. Fold a bundle of strands in half. With right side of the work facing, insert a crochet hook from the wrong side through one of the edge stitches. At the fold point, catch the bunch of strands with the hook.

2 Pull the fold through the work to the back. Take out the hook to leave a loop.

3 Using your fingers, pull the tails of the bunch of strands through the loop.

4 Pull on the tails to tighten the loop firmly and secure the tassel.

Weaving in yarn ends

It is important to weave in the tail ends of the yarn so that they are secure and your crochet won't unravel. Thread a tapestry needle with the tail end of yarn. On the wrong side, take the needle through the crochet one stitch down on the edge, then take it through the stitches, working in a gentle zigzag. Work through four or five stitches then return in the opposite direction. Remove the needle, pull the crochet gently to stretch it and trim the end.

If there are a lot of ends to weave in, I prefer to do them as I go, or the task takes ages once the crochet is complete.

How to measure a gauge square

Using the hook and the yarn recommended in the pattern, make a number of chains to measure approximately 6in (15cm). Working in the stitch pattern given for the gauge measurements, work enough rows to form a square. Fasten off.

Take a ruler, place it horizontally across the square, and using pins, mark a 4in (10cm) area. Repeat vertically to form a 4in (10cm) square on the fabric.

Count the number of stitches across, and the number of rows within the square, and compare against the gauge given in the pattern.

If your numbers match the pattern then use this size hook and yarn for your project. If you have more stitches, then your gauge is tighter than recommended and you need to use a larger hook. If you have fewer stitches, then your gauge is looser and you will need a smaller hook.

Make gauge squares using different size hooks until you have matched the gauge in the pattern, and use this hook to make the project.

Suppliers

Details of where to buy the yarns used in this book can be found through the following websites. We cannot cover all stockists here, so please explore the local yarn stores and online retailers in your own country. If you can't find the exact yarns used, your local yarn store will be able to help you find a substitute, or try the Yarnsub website for suggestions: www.yarnsub.com.

USA

LoveCrafts
Online sales
www.lovecrafts.com

Knitting Fever Inc.
www.knittingfever.com

WEBS
www.yarn.com

Jo-Ann Fabric and Craft Stores
Yarns and craft supplies
www.joann.com

Michaels
Craft supplies
www.michaels.com

UK

LoveCrafts
Online sales
www.lovecrafts.com

Wool
Yarn, hooks
Store in Bath
+44 (0)1225 469144
www.woolbath.co.uk

Wool Warehouse
Online sales
www.woolwarehouse.co.uk

Laughing Hens
Online sales
Tel: +44 (0) 1829 740903
www.laughinghens.com

John Lewis
Yarns and craft supplies
Telephone numbers of stores on website
www.johnlewis.com

Australia

Black Sheep Wool 'n' Wares
Retail store and online
Tel: +61 (0)2 6779 1196
www.blacksheepwool.com.au

Sun Spun
Retail store (Canterbury, Victoria) and online
Tel: +61 (0)3 9830 1609
www.sunspun.com.au

Mrs Moon Plump and Fluff:
www.mrsmoon.co.uk

Blue Sky Fibers: www.blueskyfibers.com

Cascade: www.cascadeyarns.com

Debbie Bliss: www.debbieblissonline.com

Drops: www.garnstudio.com

Nutscene Twine: www.nutscene.com

Rico: www.rico-design.de

Rowan: www.knitrowan.com

Sajou Metallic Thread: www.sajou.fr

Scheepjes: www.scheepjes.com

Spud & Chloë: www.blueskyfibers.com

SweetGeorgia:
www.sweetgeorgiayarns.com

West Yorkshire Spinners:
www.wyspinners.com

Index

Acknowledgments

We've had great fun with this book, which has been made possible by the lovely people who support us every day.

Most importantly, ensuring that our second book has not suffered from "tricky second album" syndrome has been our wonderful editor, Kate Haxell, who has been just as patient as ever, even considering the inclusion of charts that have given her that extra bit of work. Thank you Kate for still liking us (or pretending to anyway!); you have made it all so easy.

We must also thank the wonderfully talented Jenny Reid, who herself is an amazing crochet designer and Mrs Moon supporter and very very kindly worked up a few of the samples for us. We are very lucky to have such a kind and gifted friend!

Thank you to everyone at CICO Books, especially Cindy, Penny C (we hope we've tempted you to start crocheting), Sally, Vicky, Jo and Penny W for the beautiful design, styling and photography.

Finally, thank you to our lovely husbands, James and Tim, for all the hard work they put in to Mrs Moon behind the scenes—our new warehouse is a triumph, James! And our gorgeous children, Andrew, Florence, Ollie and Molly, Henry, Freddie (IT helpdesk!), Billy and Tilly… we'll get you making things yet!